The Church Gallery Minstrels of Old Sussex

Rev KH MacDermott

An account of the old Singers and Minstrels, the Bands, Psalmodies and Hymn-books of Sussex Churches from the end of the 17th Century to the latter half of the 19th Century published in 1922.

With an appendix on the author's collection at the Sussex Archaeological Society in Lewes and a CD of thirteen traditional Sussex carols performed by 'Hope in the Valley' recorded in 1983.

ASHRIDGE PRESS/COUNTRY BOOKS

Published by Country Books/Ashridge Press
Courtyard Cottage, Little Longstone, Bakewell, Derbyshire DE45 1NN
Tel/Fax: 01629 640670
e-mail: dickrichardson@country-books.co.uk

ISBN 978 1 901214 73 4
1 901214 73 7
© 2006 Country Books

This book was first published in 1922 as
SUSSEX CHURCH MUSIC IN THE PAST
by Moore & Wingham of Chichester.
I have made every attempt to trace the copyright holder without success.

A catalogue of titles published by Country Books and Ashridge Press
is available upon request.

Printed and bound by CPI Antony Rowe, Eastbourne

CONTENTS

John Pennicott playing the clarionet in Woodmancote Church, 1850.
From a photo of an original sketch by T. Smart, Steyning

INTRODUCTION

"No, there warn't no organ in them days. It was before the old church was pulled down and the noo one built; we had a band, up in the gallery over the big doors. Rickety old steps up to it and dark. Let's see, there was Jim Comber, the Clurk, he played the flewte; and Steve, the Cobbler, he played clar'net, and old Tomsett, Grimy Tom we called him, be scraped away on the grandmother fiddle, the bass viol y'know. An' they could play too; tarrible fine playin' twas, I rackon. I was on'y a little boy at the time, and me and my brother Tom were 'lowed to sit up in the gallery 'cos we cud sing. Us boys sung seconds and if we didn't just sing out, old Jim 'ud crack us over the head wi' his flewte. There wur 2 or 3 fiddles too and a 'horse's leg' – that's what we called the bassoon."

It was an old Sussex "musicianer" who was speaking, a patriarch of nearly 90 years of age, telling of his early reminiscences, and unveiling to me an aspect of church life of which at the time I was entirely ignorant. That was nearly thirty years ago, and as the old man was a willing and genial talker, and I was an eager listener, the story went on at some length with no interruption on my part beyond an occasional question.

"We sat up in the gallery and I used to count the winders doorin' the sarmon, whilst Gobbler wiped his clar'net dry wi' a big red han'k-erchief, and the Smith he tooned his big fiddle. No, the Passon didn't mind 'bout that; he jest kep' on a-preachin' and preachin', and when he'd done one hour he wiped his spartacles and turned the hour-glass tother way up and went on agin. Tarrible long sarmons in them days, they was! No, there warn't many books then, the Clurk he had a printed book and the singers and minstrels wrote their own books. Here's one my Feyther used, writ all by hisself. Yes, good writin' 'tis, they knew how to write then, as well as sing. Which is the melerdy? Oh ! the *air* you mean; there 'tis. Yes, the Tenor allus sung the air, not the Trebles; us boys on'y sung seconds as I was a telling on ye afore. An' when we sung out too loud, the men they glared at us and told us

5

we was a grout-headed set o' chaps. Hymn-books? No, we didn't have no 'ymns ; leastways on'y the Marnin' Hymn and one for Easter and C'ris'mas Day. We sung the Old Varsion of the Psa'ms, or sometimes the Noo Varsion, any on 'em we liked and anywhen we liked, too. No, Vicar, he didn't care what we sung and told us to bawl out what we pleased, s'longs we didn't bother him!"

Much more in the same strain was recounted to me by my old friend, and by many others of his kind in Sussex since his day. And the topic was of such never-failing interest to me that I deemed it probable that others might also like to hear the story of Sussex Church Music in the Past. All the more so inasmuch as few have ever undertaken to write a line about the subject in any of the general or local histories of the County. Music, both secular and sacred, has been neglected in Sussex literature; and Charles Fleet, in his delightful book *Glimpses of Our Ancestors* was right when he made this statement:–

"If there be one thing more conspicuous than another by its absence in the archaeological records of Sussex it is all reference to music. As a science it certainly had no existence out of the Cathedral at Chichester, in which as in all Cathedrals the practice and the tradition of an ecclesiastical school of music were kept up with more or less ability. But setting aside this ecclesiastical class of music as an exceptional and esoteric growth, scarcely touching the people, music had no existence in Sussex as a Science, and scarcely as an Art, 100 years ago. The diarists Gale, Stapley and Marchant make no mention of music ... The old and simple tunes introduced chiefly from Germany in the days of the Reformation, of which the Old 100th is almost the sole remnant, were superseded in the Stuarts' days by a more florid and pretentious kind of hymn."

This is a sweeping statement, but in the main it is unfortunately true; and it may be added that there is scarcely any reference to music in the *Sussex Archaeological Collections* or in the *Burrell MSS. (of Sussex)* at the British Museum.

Almost every branch of old church life, from episcopal visitations to "church ales," and from parsons to parish clerks; and nearly every kind of ecclesiastical art, from architecture to old brasses, has been fully treated in some work or another; but the one art that more than all others appealed to the minds of the old-time congregations, and in which they took the greatest interest, has been strangely neglected in our church literature. Unfortunately, moreover, the two main sources from which one can draw any information on the subject, and to which I have constantly turned in my reseaches during the last twenty-five years, are gradually disappearing for ever. These two sources are, first, the Old Inhabitants whose fathers and grandfathers performed and often composed the music they played; and, second, the well-thumbed and dog-eared Volumes of Music, both printed and manuscript, which were the treasured possessions of those bygone enthusiasts. And Time is relentlessly calling away the one class, while the kitchen fire is too frequently the finale of the other.

Before proceeding further it is necessary to define the term "The Past" as used in this book, otherwise the treatment of too lengthy a period of history may be anticipated by so ambiguous an expression. It is to be understood, therefore, as referring mainly to the two hundred years beginning with the latter half of the 17th and ending with the corresponding part of the 19th Century. These two hundred years cover a period in the history of Sussex church music quite distinct and separate in its characteristics from the times both before and after that period. It was an epoch indeed which differed far more widely from both its preceding and succeeding ages than these do from each other. In all departments concerned with ecclesiastical music the divergence was great: the music was different in style, the instruments were not of the same kind, the performers were in many respects dissimilar, and the places where they sang or played were at opposite ends of the churches.

For some time before The Past, as defined above, most of the church music was of a simple and stately kind as represented by the familiar *Old 100th* tune; and this was a great contrast from the florid style adopted within our period. As regards the instruments used before The Past the organ reigned practically supreme and almost alone, and it has recovered its supremacy in subsequent years; but during the time covered by the title nearly every instrument known, from a fiddle to a flute, from a trombone to a triangle, was employed;

and whereas the places in church allotted to the musicians, both before and since the period under consideration, has been in the chancel, during The Past itself it was generally up in the gallery, specially erected for the minstrels at the west end of the nave.

The whole of the local information contained in this book has been obtained by myself during my holidays and occasional sojournings in various parts of Sussex; either gleaned from the memories of the old inhabitants, or from letters sent to me by many correspondents in answer to written requests for the stories of bygone days. For some of the general information on tune-books, etc., I am indebted to Dr. A. H. Mann, of King's College, Cambridge, whose collection of old Psalmodies and kindred volumes is probably unique; and on the subject of musical instruments to the Rev, Canon F. W. Galpin, Author of *Old English Instruments of Music*, who kindly read through the manuscript of the section dealing with the Instruments.

As far as I am aware no book has hitherto appeared that has been entirely devoted to the Church Music of the Past in any particular county of England, but Canon Galpin has written *Notes on the Old Church Bands and Village Choirs of the Past Century* (chiefly relating to Dorsetshire), published in *The Antiquary,* Vol. XLII; and, in fiction, Mr. Thomas Hardy has given a delightful picture of the old Mellstock Quire (also Dorsetshire) in *Under the Greenwood Tree.*

K.H.M-D.

THE MUSICIANS

Many years ago the two parishes of Aldingbourne and Oving were held jointly by one Incumbent, who took the morning service at one church and the afternoon at the other alternately; and it was customary to have no preaching in the morning. On a certain occasion a newly-appointed Vicar expressed his intention of introducing a sermon at Matins, and he informed the choir of the proposed innovation beforehand. But the sturdy Aldingbourne singers would have "none o' his new-fangled goiogs on; they'd never 'eeard on such a thing afore and didn't see no sense to it, like." They therefore resolved to defeat the Vicar's well-meant intention. Knowing that there was never much time to spare for the Parson to have his lunch and make the journey to Oving between the two services, on the first Sunday that be went into the pulpit to preach they started singing the *119th Psalm*, and refused to stop when the would-be preacher wished. In vain the Vicar looked up at the gallery and held up his written discourse, in vain he coughed and hum'd and ha'd ; the singers would look at nothing but their "Old Version." Verse after verse they bawled out, lustily and slowly, till at last the Vicar's patience and time were completely exhausted, and he had to climb down, literally and metaphorically, and leave the Church without delivering a discourse at all!

This story (a true one) gives the key-note to the whole outlook of the old church singers and minstrels. They were whole-hearted enthusiasts for church music, and nothing would stay them from manifesting their ardour at all times. Sermons were fit and proper no doubt on "festical" occasions, but if they were preached when they were not expected and the singing ran a risk of being curtailed thereby, then it was only just that the singers should assert themselves and stand up for their rights! The "musickers" were often ignorant, sometimes without musical talent, frequently poor executants and generally somewhat irreverent; but they were always burning, and well-nigh bursting, with zeal in matters musical. They practised singing several nights a week at home or in the church; or they learned their instruments slowly and laboriously, often without any tuition save that afforded by an instruction-book or a fellow-player, devoting most of their spare time to this one and only hobby; or they spent hours of painstaking labour in the writing of volumes of manuscript music. And their enthusiasm for their tasks equalled their industry. Never, in their estimation, were there such voices anywhere as those in the Sussex church choirs; never such singers, never such players! Their daily toil was but a graceless necessity of existence: their true mission in life was to excel in the minstrels' gallery in the parish church of their native village.

About a hundred years ago one of the members of the band of Lindfield Church, a farmer named Coppard, was so energetic with his music and spent go much time in practising the violin that his son refused to learn to play any instrument whatever; and when he was asked the reason why he would not follow in his father's steps, he stated that he was afraid that music would take up so many hours that his farm would be neglected in consequence.

Perhaps some of our forefathers devoted more time than they should to their beloved art, but it is certainly a sad result of the boundless circuit of modern mental activities that the old-time enthusiasm for one definite pursuit, especially that of the church musician, is now very nearly extinct.

As already stated (in the Introduction) one of the main sources of our knowledge about the music of The Past consists of the old musicians themselves; and it will make the story more graphic, as well as authentic, if many of them are allowed to tell their reminiscences in their own ingenuous and vivid way. Copious extracts from original letters, and a few from magazines and local histories, will therefore be given in these pages to render the picture of bygone days more real and animate. Thus, Mr. Fred Jones, of East Hoathly:–

"When quite a lad I well remember being one of a band of musicians, whose ambition was to play in the district Christmas Carols (many of local creation) and anthems of Tolhurst, Figg, etc., most of them of a florid character and containing solos suited for the splendid tenor and bass voices that distinguished our assembly.

My home, a beautiful little village nestled mid the lovely beeches and elms of the thymy Downs, just before my birth had had its old church rebuilt, and the village band had to give place to a small organ with a finger-board and a barrel. The old singers lingered on for many a day and met in a large cottage on Sunday evenings. When a boy I played the flute and delighted to go to local churches to play a Te Deum or Anthem.

There were in our company 2 violins, 2 flutes, 1 oboe, 1 bassoon and bass-viol, and a 'grand-mother fiddle' as we boys used to designate her.

My father had a remarkably fine tenor voice of great compass and of exquisite sweetness. About the tame of Queen Victoria's coronation, when my father was at Brighton Theatre, a delay in the performance caused an individual to call on Tom Jones for a song. He sang so charmingly *All in the Downs* and *Tom Bowling* ..."

Speaking, or rather writing, of solos, I had a fine manuscript containing an anthem with a remarkable running bass. My brother lent it to one of the Mohawk Minstrels, and I had, I can't say the pleasure but the pain of hearing my old friend trotted out as a solo on a euphonium or some bass brass instrument! ! ! The only thing I did enjoy was the applause that followed! I never saw my old book again.

... I can recall the soft tremolo of my father's charming voice, his top notes reverberated without noise or harshness, pure and true as a bell. My brother Jude, who sang so many years at Stamner, had some of his parent's precious gifts; and used them for the Church he so loved.

I am afraid I am writing about what is gone, and perhaps haply buried in oblivion, yet I must trouble you with a type of the many carols we used to sing and play; too often I am afraid to the annoyance of the inhabitants. Once at Preston (near Brighton) we had the startling announcement by the Butler, "If you don't soon clear off, my Lady says, I am to let the Newfoundland loose!"

The experiences of the old Christmas waits were doubtless many and varied, and they had to bear much scorn and ridicule at times; but their ingenuous sayings and doings were often very droll and comical, though the humour of them was quite "unbeknownst" to themselves, and they unconsciously earned much of the ridicule levelled at them.

One Christmas Eve, in the middle of the last century, a man came to Selmeston Vicarage and began singing a Christmas hymn by himself; and as the Parson appeared at the door he felt its necessary to explain his solitude. And thus the hymn proceeded:–

> "While shepherds watched their flocks by night
> (If you please, sir, my party's all jacked up,)
> All seated on the ground,
> (There was young Harry down here,)
> The angel of the Lord came down
> (And my brother Jem and Tom and George, we've all
> bin practisin' together),
> And glory shone around.
> (But nary one on'em would come wi' me, they've all
> properly jacked up, sir!) "

To continue Mr. P. Jones' reminiscences:–

"For many years the singers and band visited the principal houses in Falmer and Stanmer, but a too generous public prevented our ever attempting again to visit neighbouring villages. About 1864 most of the old men having died our band was disbanded. Alas, they were indeed happy meetings, notwithstanding the disdain with which a more educated public regarded our old compositions with their Repeat and Twiddle.

At Stanmer and Falmer the organ was played by the honorable ladies at the Mansion. When they left home we fell back on the wretched barrel-organ. This had many evils, it could not be lightly suppressed, when once its services were employed. Occasionally we had an instrumental solo after the words were finished; but we were never so badly fixed as the good folks at Wannock were reputed to have been. Their barrel could not be silenced even when thrown into an open grave, for the tradition says it then began on its own, *All people that on earth below.*

My wife remembers the Morleys, Chowns, etc., who played at Woodmancote Church, passing her home punctually every Sunday and laden with the big fiddle; they, toiled weekly over Henfield

Common. Along the Weald from Henfield to Ditchling clever players and fine voices abounded.

As a boy I was fond of geography. Our old Clerk at Falmer had a daughter in service at a private school at Brighton. The girl gave her mother an old atlas, without covers. Her father loved *John Barleycorn* and purloined his wife's treasure, offering it to me for fifteen pence, which I was delighted to pay. The book was duly bought, and when delivered, I annoyed the old man by saying, 'Master Walls, I have paid the money to your wife!' I shall never forget the explosion that occurred: 'You bladder-headed stupid thing, you might just as well have thrown it into the ditch!'

One can almost hear the sigh of pathos in the words 'Alas, they were indeed happy meetings'; and one can echo the regret that those days have gone by for ever. Think of the painstaking and earnest industry revealed in the foregoing letter ; picture the simple-minded enthusiasts in winter toiling on foot along the muddy roads, carrying their weighty instruments with them Sunday after Sunday, to play in Churches utterly devoid of warmth or comfort, in the presence of a too-often somnolent congregation, with a parson who frequently took no interest whatever in their efforts.

The custom of visiting other adjacent churches was general; the old minstrels delighted in helping their neighbours and having an interchange of harmony. Stanmer visited Falmer, Henfield journeyed to Woodmancote, Lancing trudged to Sompting, Tarring went to Broadwater, Heathfield called on Waldron, Ferring dropped in on Goring! What the clergy said about these choral excursions I know not, but there was evidently a friendly rivalry among the old church 'musicianers,' conducive to the advantage of everyone concerned.

The youthful ambition to be a church minstrel was common and many a young fellow diligently learnt some instrument and laboriously copied out his own music by hand.

Mr. G. Marshall, of Rogate:–

"Mr. Gane has asked me to answer the letter he received from you. The first thing is best to say that I am 84 years of age. I have played different instruments in Rogate Church for 65 years, left off 6 or 7 years ago, and was presented with £50 and a silver Tea-pot.

I well remember playing when a boy with the old Band which consisted of 2 flutes, cello, 2 violins, and sometimes a clarinet. I have the concert flute that my brother used to play, the cello is got behyond repair. That broke up after a few years and then the School Master had to lead the singing and not being musical I was obliged to use a pitch-pipe, but I forget what went with it, and then followed a barrel-organ which I played for some time and then an harmonium for a few years and at last the organ, which I played untill I gave it up. I remember the music was all MS. Many of the tunes used were the same as are used at the present time. *Hanover, Old Hundredth, Abridge, Manchester New* and *Mariners* which was always used at the beginning of the Morning Services, and only 4 verses were ever sung no matter the length of the hymn."

The custom of using one particular hymn and tune at the commencement of the service every Sunday was general, and the congregations do not seem to have wearied of this somewhat monotonous usage. Our forefathers were indeed contented with a very little variety in either words or music. Wm. Gresham in *Psalmody Improved* (published about 1780) states that he 'has limited the number of tunes in the book to 40, because if more were inserted the Congregation could not retain them;' and the book issued in 1761 for the Charity Children of Chichester (see Ch.iii.) ends its introduction thus:– "Here are thirteen, plain, good tunes, and thirty-nine Portions of some of the most useful Parts of the Psalms: If three Psalms be allowed to each Sunday, the Collection will be sung through once a Quarter." In the days when few of our forefathers could rend they had to learn the Psalms by heart if they wished to sing, and a paucity of both tunes and psalms in a book was almost necessary, but the monotony must have been extreme.

The practice of limiting the number of verses sung to four, no matter bow long the hymn or psalm, was common and was doubtless intended to neutralise the lengthy pulpit discourses; but a good many spiritual songs must have become somewhat unintelligible in this curtailing process. Some of the compilers of the old metrical Psalm-odies recognised the custom and selected four verses only of each psalm that they used in their publications, with a more edifying result than could have obtained when the choir always sang merely the first four verses indiscriminately.

Reference is frequently made in the reminiscences of the old choir-men to the days when there 'warn't no scholards' among their number and the psalms and anthems were learnt by heart.

"We used to have what you call a String Choir; there was one bass viol, 2 violins, a flute, and what we called a spoke-pipe to start the singing; and each singer took certain parts and they would join in altogether and there was one old man who could neither read or write but he used to be almost the leader. I don't think there is one of the singers living only my eldest brother and he is 84 years old now. He can still sing the old anthems with his eyes shut."

Such feats of memory were common in the benighted days of our forefathers. At Twineham, about 80 years ago, the leader of the choir was quite illiterate, but he managed to conduct the other singers as well as to take his own part. A few years ago, a well-known ringer and singer, named Henry Burstow, died at Horsham, who could sing 400 of the old Sussex and other folk-songs by heart. Many of the old psalm-tunes were of a florid nature, full of 'repeats and twiddle,' and they were a greater task for the memory than modern hymn-tunes are; but by assiduous practice the minstrels mastered them with more or less efficiency.

Most of the bands had a leader, who acted as conductor as well, but as he always played an instrument himself his control over the *tempo* of the music was often scarcely adequate, and a break-down was not uncommon, especially at the start. At Lurgashall 'there was a Church band which ceased to exist about 1840,' and the mainstay of it was one George Sadler who died in 1838. The Sunday after his death the band broke down and was 'never no sense afterwards.' But the singing was carried on unaccompanied for some years – 'Someone used to start a tune and the rest on us came in!'

The minstrels usually performed in the gallery at the west end of the nave; these galleries were often erected specially for their use, and the right to sit in them, as will be shown later was jealously guarded. There is a charming picture entitled *The Village Choir*, by T. Webster, in the Victoria and Albert Museum, wherein the Artist has depicted a

15

gallery scene in former days. There are the singers, men in smocks or broadcloth, girls in poke-bonnets; among them are the players of the clarionet, bassoon and bass-viol, while the conductor, or leader, is at a desk in front beating time with his hand.

When there was no gallery the musicians performed in some convenient place in the nave; they rarely seem to have occupied the chancel. At Selsey they stood in the front pew, and had a high desk attached to the front of the pew for their music; the notches and screw-holes where the iron arms supporting the desk were fastened may still be seen in the woodwork of the pew (which is now the 5th one on the north side of the nave). At Boxgrove the band for a time stood round the pulpit; but when the gallery was available they migrated to the loftier position. The present Duke of Richmond has related that he remembers hearing the band in his boyhood's days, and that as soon as the minstrels commenced to play, the whole congregation turned round and 'faced the music' and remained in that attitude until the singing ceased.

At Birdham there was an irascible old man who played the violin and put more warmth of expression into his performance than was desirable at times. On one occasion during a service when he was doing his musical best, a fiddlestring broke, arousing bis passions beyond control. In his fury he flung his instrument down from the gallery into the body of the church and shouted: "Goo down there and bide there!" And he refused to play any more.

The Parish Clerk at Aldingbourne sat in bis wonted place under the pulpit during the first part of the service, but he always went up into the gallery to join in the anthem, for "they couldna a-got along 'ithout 'im, in coorse"! After the 1st Collect he loudly said *Amen* from the pulpit's 'lower deck'; at the end of the 2nd Collect his *Amen* came less audibly as he strode down the nave; and the third *Amen* was heard by the congregation in a muffled and distant tone from the hidden stair-way leading to the gallery!

The best evidence for the jealousy that existed in reference to the sitting in the gallery is given in the *Cuckfield Book* (a volume containing the chronicles of the parish for the past two or three centuries) wherein is recorded a most elaborate set of rules for the singers and the persons privileged to sit in the gallery, drawn up in 1699. Some extracts from this book are here given:–

"Rules agreed on by the Vicar and divers of the chief of the Parishioners and other persons that contributed to the Building of the New Gallery for singing Psalms for ye better order of those that sitt and sing in it.

Impr: [Imprimis] This Gallery being built only for ye singing of Psalms by those yt have learnt, and for their singing ym together, therefore tis agreed that it be used by such only (and those allowed to be Good or Competent Singers by ye major part of the Quire) and by no other, tho' Proprietor, till approved Singers.

2. That Timothy Burrell, Esq., (who gave 2£ 00s 00d) Wm. Board, Esq (who gave 3£) Bob. Middleton, Vicar (who gave both for work and materials, and for ye Faculty from the Bishop at least 4£i … [and others'] … have the five or six inner places in the Front seate on the right hand for ye Principall Bass, if they be singers, and according to their Bank. And that the two outer places be for Tenours wch two at present are Samuel Savage, Yeoman, (who gave 01£i 10s) and Charles Savage, Yeoman, his Brother (who also gave 01£i 10s).

(Rules 3 to 8 contain 'instructions for the seating of everyone according to rank, the "inferiour proprietors" to go into the "next best places" and the women and maidservants to yield place to their "Betters.")

9. Since ye Singers are a running body and sometimes a family of ye Proprieters may have more or less, or none that can sing well, and since if they all had a competent number of Singers there would not be enough places for ym … they must take their lott without murmuring.

(Rules 10 to 14 contain further instructions for Proprieters, the Clerk, for disposal of seat at death, and as to behaviour of juveniles.

15. That as ye Bishop enjoyns in his Faculty divers of the Singers … disperse themselves in the congregation … to assist others to sing.

(Rules 16 to 18 refer to disputes, safekeeping of this book, etc.)

Signatures:–　　Tim Burrell.
　　　　　　　　Will Board
　　　　　　　　Bob. Middleton, Vicar,(and 19 others).

In *An Old Wealden Village* (1903) by Miss E. Bell-Irving the author gives an extract from the Archbishop's Faculty for the Erection of the Minstrels' Gallery in Mayfield in 1731:–

"Whereas Bob. Hooper, Vicar and the principal inhabitants of the said parish are desirous to promote the singing of the Psalms in the said Church to the honour of Almighty God in the most decent and orderly manner, and do judge that a gallery ... will be convenient to answer to that end. ... Wee have granted licence and authority to erect ... a gallery for the sole use of such persons who shall sing Psalms skilfully and well. ... And we further order that some of the singers doe sometimes disperse themselves into the body of the Church for the direction and assistance of such persons as shall have a pious intention of learning to sing."

The privilege of sitting in the minstrels' gallery was obviously reserved for the few; and apparently the singers were encouraged to regard themselves as among the elect in the musical portions of the service, at whose feet the ordinary members of the congregation had to sit and humbly learn.

It is often said that the natives of Sussex are not musical, but that is only a comparative truth. They have not had the chances for learning music that the people in the crowded north have had, nor are they possessed of such musical voices as are the Welsh; but the inborn desire to hear music, and also the ambition to express themselves in song, is far more widespread and real among Sussex folk than is generally supposed. Many a humble cottage have I known wherein Bill or Tom 'scrapes a bit on the fiddle' or 'plays a bit to hisself, like!'; or in which Jim or Mary can sing 'well 'nough to join in a chorus.' Their opportunities for receiving good instruction have been rare and their musical accomplishments have consequently not been great, but throughout Sussex there is or has been, a large amount of latent talent and partially trained skill. The old Church minstrels were certainly keen, if not altogether competent, musicians; and there was a general desire on the part of the average members of the congregations to have musical services.

This desire has often shown itself in ways that evoke a smile nowadays. In the middle of the 19th century the people of Westhampnett 'counted it an enviable privilege to go to Oving Church to hear the barrel-organ there.' At another church crowds assembled to hear the new instrument called the 'harmonium!' At Egdean the congregation used to sit and sing Psalms by themselves while they waited before the service for the coming of the parson. On one occasion a new "minister" arrived at the church and found the congregation singing away lustily; he waited till they had finished and then exclaimed – "I see you are all having a jollification without pipe or pot!"

The old-time zeal for music sometimes made discretion a laggard. The eagerness on the part of the Mayfield choir, not only to sing, but to choose their music as well, led to an unseemly incident on one occasion. "The clerk, who was the chief musician, and the singers were at variance as to the tunes to be used. Before any musical portion of the service he left his seat below the pulpit and ascended to the gallery to play the accompaniments. So strained were the relations between himself and the singers that on one particular Sunday, when he played his chosen tune, dead silence prevailed among them; if they could not sing as they wished they would not sing at all. The following Sunday instead of mounting the stairs he stood below the gallery and called up to them, 'Be ye agoing to sing to-day or hain't ye? Because if ye hain't agoing to sing I hain't agoing to play!' "

About twenty-five years ago I went to preach at one of the tiny Wealden churches, tucked away under the shadow of the swelling Downs, wherein the choirmaster was justly proud both of his own voice and of the singing of the choir. It was the morning service and while the chant for the *Venite* was being played, he glanced across the chancel at me with a look that plainly said, 'Now you will hear some chanting worth hearing.' Unfortunately in his fervour he forgot which canticle was to be sung and while the other members of the choir started "O come, let us sing," he sang out at the top of his voice, "My soul doth magnify the Lord!" They fought it out lustily for two verses; the one for the *Magnificat*, the others for the *Venite*; then there was a complete collapse of the singing altogether. I did my best to cover up the confuaion by singing the *Venite* where the breakdown occurred, but the choir and their leader were very subdued through the remaining verses of that canticle.

This incident served to illustrate the zeal of the Sussex musician even in a degenerate age of church minstrelsy, and before the end of the service the pleasure I derived from the hearty singing quite outweighed the dismay caused by the initial mishap.

There can be little doubt that the ardour of our forefathers as regards the music of the Sunday services kept awake a great deal of native musical talent in Sussex that would otherwise have been dormant; and it is a misfortune in some respects that the professional performer is now so much more available, even in remote villages, than he used to be. Many who might have become singers or players themselves are now content to do nothing but listen; and some are fallen so low that music has to be accompanied by moving pictures to make any appeal to their debased minds at all!

Canon Irton Smith, of West Grinstead, in a letter written to me in 1917 expressed himself strongly in this manner:

"I hold that England's decline in musical ability, reputation and interest, dates from the expulsion of these old church bands by the newly-invented (anti-musical) harmonium. Before that, each instrument in the gallery practically guaranteed one household interested in music and preserving traditions. Now, the 'flaxen headed ploughboy that whittles o'er the lea' owes all his melody to the music-hall."

This is a stern indictment of the present days, but it is largely true as regards country villages and small towns, wherein the musical talent of a few only is cultivated, while a great many persons who might become moderate performers make no attempt to learn music at all. Thus there has been some progress among a small minority, but the bulk of the population has retrograded. In large towns where schools of music and other facilities for the cultivation of the art abound, England has certainly advanced very considerably both in ability and reputation in music.

Opinions as to the merits of the voices of the Sussex choirmen of The Past have been widely divergent; no praise was too high on the one hand, no contempt too great on the other. The eulogies were generally bestowed on each other by the singers themselves – all honour to them for their loyalty to their fellows – while the scorn was heaped upon the vocalists, without measure, by the compilers of tune-books or by non-vocal members of the congregations. As a matter of fact I believe that both parties were somewhat biassed, and neither the praise nor the blame was wholly deserved.*

The judgment of the singers upon their companions is pleasant reading and shall be recorded first. As quoted before Mr. Fred Jones, states:– "Along the weald from Henfield to Ditchling clever players and fine voices abounded."

Mr. G. W. Ashby, of Wadhurst, says:– "I have heard Uncle William mention that in his young days the Wadhurst choir boasted of having two of the best and most powerful voices in England, this of course was saying much, the two names were Cooper and Luard, tenor and bass. I have beard my Uncle sing bass, it was a very strong deep tone but he acknowledged it was nothing compared to Cooper. Uncle must have been the last of the Band, he passed away about 1897 and was then 84."

Withyham church had 'musical services above the average of country churches for many years.' Mr. F. Stroud, of Hellingly:– "In the olden days four brothers, Charles, Stephen, Edward and another Colbran sang in the choir. Besides them was Jesse Dunk, a fine bass singer and Thomas Gilbert another bass with a wonderful voice who used to give out the Hymns and Anthems. The leader of the choir was John Francis Richardson who on leaving the parish in 1843 was presented by the Rev. John Olive, Vicar, and the Congregation, with a beautiful silver snuff-box gilt-lined which I have seen as it is in the posssssion of his daughter. ... In those days Hellingly was the best choir in the neighbourhood."

Mr. W. J. Harris, of Donnington, wrote of other matters besides the fine voices of the choirmen; but his description of the parish in olden days is too graphic to be curtailed:–

"Mrs. Davis thought I might be able to tell you something about the old church music at Donnington. I am afraid I know but very little. I have heard my Father say there was no music in the Church up to

---

* The chapter on tune-books, etc., will show the usual attitude of mind of the compilers of Psalmodies and Hymn-books towards the singing of the average church choir.

1840. About that time or soon after, the Parson got together a choir and some instruments, a violin, a clarinet and one or two flutes and sometime later a bass and 'cello. Principally members of the Davis family, these gradually died out till in about 1855 the only one left was old William Davis and his flute. He continued playing till about his death in 1868. The choir then had the middle row of seats opposite the school children. I can remember back to 1864. The choir then were old Edward Davis, his sons Godfrey, Tom and George, Tom aad Charles Shepherd from North End, William Powell and William Osmond, Miss Anne Davis and about fifteen girls of the Poore, Arnell, Shepherd, Beech and Powell families. Tom Davis had a very fine voice and would have gone high in the singing world but for his drinking habits. W. Osmond was leading tenor in the Cathedral for many years. It was said at the time that the singing was the best of any village church in the County. Mr. Stansfield (Vicar) bought the first harmonium to the church in 1868.

At the early part of the last Century, Donnington had the reputation of being the most blackguard parish in the County, there were several noted smuggling families in the place; I think everyone had something to do with it more or less. Some of the old men have told me that many a cargo of tubs and tobacco has been stored in the Church and in the Fogden vault near the Church door, and the girls were such noted characters that it was dangerous for any young man to be out after dark. If caught he was stripped or had to pay to get free. Fortunately a succession of remarkably good Clergy, Mr. Daniells, Mr. Kenrich and Mr. Stansfield, worked a great improvement and Mr. Crobie acquiring the whole of the parish and living at Northlands was a great benefit, a dozen or more of the very bad old houses were pulled down, a little school was started in a loft at Pelleys, and later the present school was built. Donnington became the third best conducted parish in England. The general habits of people are much improved, but the present men and women are not to be compared to those of my early days. What a grand lot they were. I shall always remember them with esteem and respect."

Donnington's resurgence from such a low state of morality to the honourable position of the third best conducted parish in England is praiseworthy, but one wonders how it failed to attain either the first or second place, and what were the names of those places more worthy than itself? Let us hope they were also in Sussex!

Usually the self-applause, often well justified, of the old minstrels was reserved for conversation out of Church, but on one occasion the singing was apparently so good that the leader of the choir was unable to restrain his feelings to the end of the service:– "Vicissitudes occurred in the musical portion of the services in this [West Tarring] Church after the removal of the old 18th century organ, the parishioners from time to time forming bands to supply its place. The orchestra formed in the early part of last century, consisting of bass-viols, bassoons, hautbois and flutes, was not spoken of in very flattering terms by those of the then old inhabitants with whom I was intimately acquainted in my youthful days, although it appears to have given satisfaction to the performers themselves; as on one occasion when Henry Polling, then of the Fig Gardens, was conductor, he, at the end of an anthem in order to show his appreciation of the performance, struck his baton sharply on the gallery, and shouted out, Well done, lads!" (*Transcripts and Records of the Past*, by Ed. Sayers.)

It was well, perhaps, that the old choirmen were satisfied as a rule with their own performances, for very few writers on the subject of Church music in The Past ever had much praise for them, and scathing criticisms of both the singing and playing are frequent in the books of the period, not as regards Sussex only, but in reference to England in general. Thos. Mace in *Music's Monument* (1676) in allusion to the Psalm singing of the day, says, "It is sad to hear what whining, yelling and screeching there is in many congregations, as if the people were affrighted or distracted."

Most of the prefaces or introductions to the numerous psalm-tune books issued during the 18th Cent. contain adverse criticisms of the way in which the Psalms were rendered at the time; and the compilers of such books (as will be seen from the extracts given later on) nearly always declared that the object of their works was to improve the musical portions of the church services.

J. A. La Trobe in *The Music of the Church* (1831) expresses himself strongly concerning the attitude of the clergy of his day towards the musical part of the services:–

"It were vain to endeavour to cloak the indifference with which they generally regard this part of their duty, to superintend, regulate and inspirit the music of the church. In most places the choir are left to their own fitful struggles, without any offer of clerical assistance. Occasionally, a native admiration of the art, a vague sense of obligation, a fondness for power, or a spirit of interference, operating severally or collectively, may arouse to exertion. But obstacles arise at every step, taste is outraged, dignity is offended, zeal is soon Humbled, and the attempt to regulate [the music] is abandoned as hopeless. ... It is to be feared, that in most parishes, no other kind of attention [than that of wanton interference by the parson] is even imagined as obligatory on the part of the minister. To this almost general neglect may be mainly attributed the present infirm state of sacred music throughout the kingdom."

La Trobe further describes the attitude of the parson towards the singing at the time when he is about to preach, when he goes into the vestry to doff his surplice and don the blackgown for the sermon:–

"The solemn liturgy is concluded. After a moment's silent prayer, all rise from their knees, their minds prepared for the cheering invitation, 'Let us sing to the praise and glory of God.' The psalm is given out. The singers elbow themselves into notice, and the tune advances. Verse follows verse – but he appointed to lead the public devotions is no longer in his place in the house of God. At last the vestry door opens, the eyes of the people follow him up the aisle, and are hardly recalled to their duty, till he has ascended the pulpit. Hitherto he has rather disturbed, than countenanced this portion of the service. After a moment's pause; a few lines perhaps remain, during the singing of which, as a last redeeming effort, he may yet encourage by the sound of his voice or the movement of his lips, the hallowed exercise of praise. No, it is time that he has to spare – and looking once round upon the congregation, he sits back upon his seat, there reposing till the wearisome duty is performed."

La Trobe's remarks no doubts applied as fitly to the Sussex clergy in former days as to others; and I have not gathered much evidence to contravert the charge. The zeal for church music, the management of the choir and band, the provision of music and instruments, the conduct of practices and the general maintenance of the singing, seems to have been confined to the singers and players themselves. The clergy posed as critics, rather than helpmates; and the congregations too often followed suit.

In Thomas Hardy's delightful story of the old church minstrels in a Dorsetshire village, in *Under the Greenwood Tree*, a most amusing description of an old parson and his indifference to the music of the church is given. "Yes; he was a right sensible, pa'son," said Michael. "He never entered our door but once in his life, and that was to tell my poor wife that as she was such a' old aged person, and lived so far from the church he didn't at all expect her to come any more to the service. And 'a was a very jinerous gentleman about choosing the psalms and hymns o' Sundays. 'Confound ye,' says he, 'blare and scrape what ye will, but don't bother me!' "

Mr. Edward Sayers in *Transcripts and Records of the Past*: West Tarring, gives a vivid picture of church music in bygone days and of the attitude of parson and choir towards each other:– "Early in the 'thirties' James Newman, who came to reside in this parish from Nuthurst, where he used to play the clarionet in the church, formed a band consisting of himself as leader, clarionet; T. Binstead, bass-viol; Ch. Bushby, trombone; Ch. and T. Chipper, bassoons; J. and G. Chipper, clarionets. This orchestra of farm-labourers, wearing pure white smock-frocks, together with the choristers, then called the Psalm-singers, sat in the gallery, and continued in existence down to within a few years of the restoration of the church; when this was completed in 1854, an organ was purchased and placed in the tower, a choir was formed of which I was one of the first members; we sat in the tower men, women, boys and girls, all singing in unison, and to the backs of the congregation. After a few years some of the choir formed a choral class for the purpose of learning and introducing harmony into the church. The organist being away on a holiday, and having to sing without accompaniment we thought it a good opportunity to try a hymn in four parts. *The Old Hundredth* was selected for the first, and to be sung when the Vicar went into the vestry to change his surplice for his gown, in which to preach the sermon, as was the custom in those days. I was to blow the note with a pitch-pipe; this I did, and all took up and sustained their parts well. The congregation turned round and faced us, *en masse*. The Vicar came out of the vestry looking with astonishment, and as black as the gown he bad just put on, and immediately dispatched his clerk with a message for our leader, Henry Overington, to attend in the vestry at the end of the service. Seeing the Vicar was displeased with the innovation, the hymn at the end of the service was sung in the usual way. Our leader, as desired, went into the vestry and the rest of the choir awaited the verdict. On his return, he stated that the Vicar asked him what we were singing, our leader said:– 'I told him we were singing the *Old Hundredth* in four parts and I thought it went very well.' The Vicar replied, 'I don't profess to know much about music, it might have gone very well, but don't do it again.'

Little clusters gathered together on their way home after the service discussing the merits, or the demerits, of the singing. One old man said to another:– 'What was the matter with the singers to-day, then?' The other replied:– 'I dunno, some was singen one toon and some was singen another, and Edward Sayers was gwain to play some sort of instrument, but he broke down fust noat.' So we continued in unison with our singing, as well as with our Vicar, for some years longer."

Mr. Sayers' mother (born 1803) said she did not like the singing because the altos sang through their noses.

The Vicar of West Tarring was one whose "taste was outraged and dignity offended," but he expressed himself less harshly than did Dr. Burton, who in his Journal (1750) writes in reference to Church Psalmody at Shermanbury:– "The more shrill-toned they [the Sussex people] may be, the more valued they are, and in Church they sing Psalms, by preference, not set to the old and simple tune, but as if in a tragic chorus, changing about in strophe and anti-strophe, and stanzas with good measure ; but yet there is something offensive to my ear when they bellow to excess and bleat out some goatish noise with all their might."

The last remark was probably true of most of the old Sussex choirs, to whom the term piano had little meaning and for whom *pianissimo* most certainly never existed. The choir at Willingdon in the middle of last century consisted of 'a lot of young men who sang, or *bawled* unaccompanied.'

In the Parish Register of Buxted occurs the following quaint entry:– 'The old Clerk of this Parish, who had continued in the office of Clerke and Sexton for the space of 43 yeares, whose melody warbled forth as if he had been thumped on the back by a stone, was buried 20th September, 1666.'

A reference to the singing at Twineham early last century:– 'The bandsmen and choirmen were of the peasant class; they assembled occasionally in each others cottages for a practice. Some of them were quite unable to read and had learnt the Anthems from hearing them sung by others; and the result must have been more interesting than edifying.'

Perhaps the most scathing comment on the singing of any choir was made by the famous iron-master, John Fuller, M.P., who lived at Brightling a century ago. He presented nine *bassoons* to the minstrels of the village church in order that they might drown the voices of the choir! (What this meant will be realised from the fact that the sound of the bassoon has often been likened to the braying of an ass, and Beethoven in his *8th Symphony* gives a passage to the bassoons in octaves which seems intended to imitate that animal's vocal efforts.)

There can be little doubt that the singing in olden days was more lusty than refined, more original than artistic, more vigorous than tuneful; but the whole-hearted efforts of the devoted musicians largely made up for a lack of knowledge and skill. There was a simple directness about their voluntary labours which makes one regret the bygone days.

The manners and customs of the old singers were often delightfully simple and primitive, especially in the matter of dress:–

"I have try'd to remember the Old Choir at Climping where we live'd many years and generations before us, in our early childhood we attended our dear Old Church and can remember the Blacksmith and his Son playing the Violins and the Churchwarden the Bassvial and two others the Shoemakers play'd a flute each they all wore

White-Smock-frock and carried their Instruments and manuscript Music in a *Red-Hanker-chiefs* but none of these Old relics can be found."

The smock-frock was a very sensible and useful garment and its disuse is a sign of the foolish craving for modernity on the part of our country-folk, who would be much happier and more picturesque if they clung more closely to many of the old fashions. The cboirmen in their white smocks were far more in keeping with the grey old Sussex churches than are their cassocked and surpliced successors of today.

When the famous John Fuller presented the barrel-organ to Brightling Church, before the days of his displeasure at the singing, he gave each male member of the choir a smock-frock, buckskin breeches and yellow stockings; and to each woman a red cloak.

The custom of wearing a red cloak was observed by the female members of the West Lavington choir up to recent years. It arose in 1849 when the church was built, and the costumes were given by the first Vicar of the parish. Rev. J. Currie. The cloaks were scarlet, trimmed with black braid, and white sun-bonnets were worn with them. Owing to the red cloaks becoming shabby and worn out, blue ones have recently been substituted for them.

At Goring, the schoolgirls helped in the singing and responses with the Clerk, and they wore white straw poke-bonnets, trimmed with white cambric, and pink and white print dresses and capes.

Thinking of the garments of the choirs reminds me of an incident that took place in Sussex, and although it has no reference to music it is worthy of record.

During the Commonwealth the Vicar of Egdean was a popular man, and the Cromwellian Puritans found it a difficult matter to oust him out of the living as they wished. In most parishes the parsons had to leave their benefices during this period owing to the "religious fervour" of the Roundheads, who seized upon any excuse to drive the Clergy out, and then substituted "intruded ministers" of their own. One Sunday the Vicar of Egdean was climbing over a gate and in doing so burst a button off his breeches. He stopped at a cottage and asked a woman to sew it on again, and for this he was charged with *breaking* the sabbath and turned out of his living.

One of the happy features of the old church minstrelsy was the common custom of whole families for generations taking part therein, the juniors regarding it almost a sacred obligation that they should carry on the traditions of their ancestors in this respect. There was no compulsion about it, however, and the obligation was generally regarded as a privileged one. Notable instances of the custom may be given. At Bosham the family of Arnold supplied members of the choir without a break for nearly 90 years; at Falmer the Jones and Sandall families did the same for a long period; the Cootes at Clymping, the Hodges and Roberts at Henfield and Shermanbury, the Collins and Unsteads at Waldron, the Marshalls at Rogate, the Sayers, Bushby, Binstead and Chipper families at West Tarring, the Ashbys at Wadhurst, the Ransomes at Sidlesham – all these had many members of different generations in their respective church choirs; while at Donnington the band at one time was formed by twelve brothers named Davis. A. Welch was in Bosham choir in 1796 and a descendant was in it nearly a century later.

When the gallery of Aldinghourne Church was pulled down in 1890 a paper was found behind the gallery containing a register of the choirmen's attendances in 1808. The names of the singers were – T. Collins, H. G. Collins, Edmund Collins – Burnand, T. Burnand, S. Farenden, W. Willard, Goatcher, B. Pbillips, W. Maidlaw, J. Fallick, Brown.

Besides this 'family membership' of choirs a feature of The Past was the lengthy tenure of office of individual members of bands or choirs, many of whom could claim from 40 to 50 years service to their credit. At one time all the twelve adult singers at Bosham Church had an average of over 40 years continuous membership of the choir; and the senior of them, 'Grandsire' Arnold, established a record by occupying his seat for 82 years, from 1829 to 1911.

Some of the old players were tireless in their energies, not a few of them being able to play two or more different instruments. A famous character in and around Henfield in the fifties of last century was one Pennicott (or Penniket) whose performances on both clarionet and trombone were noted. A humorous sketch of him in Woodmancote Church was made by the late Mr. H. Smith, of Henfield, in which Mr.

Pennicott is depicted playing the clarionet for the anthem *Awake, thou that sleepest,* thus disturbing the slumbers of the nodding congregation.

Another accomplished musician, Mr. George Marshall, of Rogate, played several instruments and was associated with his parish church as a performer for 65 years. Mr. Marshall's father and two brothers were all good musicians, and the family spent many an hour in playing quartets together.

As far as I have been able to ascertain the old minstrels were seldom or never paid for their services; nor indeed is it the custom at the present time in Sussex for adult members of choirs to be paid. An annual 'outing' is usually the only practical return for their work that they ever receive. Occasionally a Parish Clerk was granted a little addition to his salary for acting as organist. At Bishopstone the clerk received the munificent stipend of £1 a year for 'grinding' out the music in the church, and a boy was paid 6s. a year for blowing. Evidently the churchwardens of Bishopstone determined that the poverty of the Church mouse should find a sympathetic equal in the penury of the Church Muse.

In 1762 the sum of £1 5s. 6d. was paid at Hailsham 'for peoples learning to sing in the Church.'

Not many children seem to have been employed in the old choirs, but when they were the methods adopted by the seniors to keep them in order were original if not exactly reverent. 'Grandsire' Arnold joined the Bosham choir in 1829 at the age of ten, and when he was a lad he sat near the clarinet player, and if he stopped singing for a moment, or sang softly, the bandsman would push the bell of his instrument into young Arnold's face and blow a mighty and wrathful blast at him, heedless of the musical effect produced thereby.

At Eastergate "the singing was led by the Schoolmaster playing on a flute unsupported by any other instrument (in the fifties). If any choirboy misbehaved the Schoolmaster would stop playing, correct the offender with the flute, and resume; whether the congregation waited during the performance my father cannot remember."

At Cuckfield it was enjoined in 1699 (see Rules on page 16) that "the Sidesmen do carefully overlook the youths or other members of the Quire, and either moderately correct them or complain to their parents, if they are guilty of playing, talking or other disorders." What the Cuckfield Sidesmen deemed to be "moderate correction" is not revealed, but in one Sussex Church it consisted in a smart blow on the offender's head with the clarinet.

In *Kipling's Sussex*, by B. Thurston Hopkins, an amusing reminiscence of the late Rev. J. C. Egerton formerly Rector of Burwash, Sussex, is given: "At the Bell Inn I met the sexton ... He was very communicative and recollected the days when the Rev. J. Egerton played the fiddle at the choir practices back in 1870. 'He had a hem o'trouble with the boys,' the old man drawled, 'and the only way he could make 'em behave reasonable like was to crack 'em on the head with his fiddle-stick. He was old-fashioned, no bounds, was the old Rector.' "

Many of the choirmen were quite irreverent in the olden days and their leaders often corrected them with outspoken and very audible rebukes. One village choir-master was often annoyed because the men sometimes sang bass or tenor or the melody of a tune indiscriminately. His exasperation reached such a pitch on one occasion that he called out just before a psalm – "If you want to sing bass, sing bass; if you want to sing tenor, sing tenor; but don't let us have none of your shandy-gaff!"

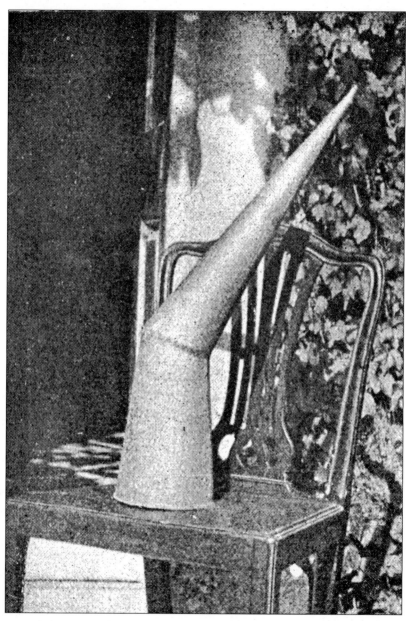

Vamphorn at Ashurst, Sussex

THE INSTRUMENTS

Any of the sins of their generations are visited on the heads of the great men of every age, and Oliver Cromwell was a notable exemplar of this historic fact. Much evil is attributed to him of which he was guiltless both in act and intention. Every visitor to a Cathedral or noteworthy Church is familiar with the usually unchallenged statement: "Cromwell destroyed this or that," and almost every iconoclastic deed of the fanatics among the Puritans has been attributed directly to the masterful Protector, including the wholesale destruction of church organs. In justice to his memory it is but fair to state that he was a good amateur musician; that he was especially fond of the organ and had one set up in Hampton Court Palace for his own pleasure; and that he constantly endeavoured to check the destructive excesses of his followers, and on most occasions counselled moderation and tolerance (see Morley's *Life of Cromwell*), In all probability, therefore, our Sussex musician, Mr. Henry Davey, of Brighton, was quite correct when he wrote to *Notes and Queries* (9th Series, Vol. Ill, 1899) defending Cromwell's memory in the matter of church organs and their destruction. It is true that they were abolished from English churches by a law passed by Parliament in 1644, and the method adopted in carrying out the law was too often riotous and sacrilegious destruction but this was not by Cromwell's own wishes or orders.

The ravage of Chichester Cathedral and the destruction of its organ by the Parliamentarians is thus described by Dean Byves: "The next day their first business was to plunder the Cathedral Church. They left not so much as a cushion for the pulpit, nor a chalice for the Blessed Sacrament. The commanders having in person executed the covetous part of the sacrilege they leave the destructive and spoiling part to be finished by the common soldiers. As they broke down the organ and dashed the pipes with their pole axes they cried out in scoff, 'Harke how the organs goe'!" Cromwell was not present at the capture of Chichester, the Parliament troops being led by Waller, and Sussex at any rate cannot lay the destruction of its Cathedral organ to his charge.

The Puritan rage against music and organs was not a bitter hatred of the instruments or music *per se*, but was rather a righteous indignation at the frivolous manner of the singing in vogue in the days of Charles I. As a matter of fact the Puritans were fond of music and evinced it by their frequent Psalm-singing; moreover in 1656 a Committee of Council was formed to assist in founding a College of Music in London, a project that was only stopped by the Restoration in 1660!

Whoever was responsible, however, it is actually true that from the middle of the 17th Century to the corresponding part of the 19th there were very few churches (other than Cathedrals, Collegiate Chapels, etc.) wherein the instrumental part of the music was provided by an organ (excluding barrel-organs from the category for the moment). The Cathedrals and some of the larger town churches began to be provided with organs soon after the Restoration, but small village churches remained without them as a rule until the latter half of the 19th Century. Direct evidence of this is furnished by the Selsey *Collection of Psalms* where the Preface, which was written in 1842, makes this statement:–

"The Organ, it must be allowed, adds much to the effect of Church Music and by a peculiarly ready construction it is now brought within the range of economy (however limited) of every parish. Its general adoption is therefore strongly recommended and earnestly to be hoped for. – Selsey, September 30th, 1842."

In the absence of organs the singing was usually unaccompanied, the starting note being given on a pitchpipe, until the end of the 18th Century, when there came the general introduction of bands of various instruments. Nearly every church in Sussex had its band at one time, the members of it being the local villagers, who generally owned, as well as played, their instruments. These bands seem to have flourished very well till the fatal advent of the harmonium or American organ brought about their doom.

In the County there were no less than 24 different kinds of musical instruments employed in one church or another, *viz*:– Banjo, Barrel-organ, Bass-horn, Bassoon, Clarionet, Concertina, Cornet, Corno-pean, Double-bass, Drum, Fife, Flute, Fluteina, French-horn, Kettle-drum (or Side-drum?) Oboe, Pitchpipe, Seraphim, Serpent, Triangle, Trombone, Vamp-horn, Violin, Violoncello.

Unique amongst them all, and hardly worthy of the name of musical instrument, was the VAMP-HORN, formerly used in the church at Ashurst, where it is still preserved. This curious instrument is a single tube made of tin, 3ft in length by 7 inches across the bell or larger end. It is painted green and bears an inscription in yellow lettering: "Praise Him upon ye Strings and Pipe, 1770, Palmer fecit." Inside the bell, about $8^{1}/_{2}$ inches from the end, are stretched several intersecting wires the purpose of which is difficult to tell. They are too thick to vibrate, so cannot have been intended to increase the tone by sounding sympathetic notes. Possibly they were intended to prevent the insertion of any obstruction in the narrow part of the tube; or they may have been placed to allow a cloth to be put into the bell as a mute for special soft effects. The mouthpiece is missing; probably it was made of wood (as in the Vamp-horn at Charing in Kent) and it would in course of time easily become loose and slip off.

There are in existence five other Vamp-horns in England – at Willoughton in Lincolnshire, East Leake and Braybrooke Notting-hamshire, Charing in Kent and Harrington in Northamptonshire. All of these are larger than the Ashurst example, the one at East Leake being 7ft. 9in. in length, Various opinions have been expressed as to the purpose of these Vamp-horns, but their name seems to imply that they were used as megaphones to amplify the sound of the voices; or to assist the band in a similar manner.

The word "vamp" is derived from the French *avant-pied*, which was originally applied to the piece of leather attached to the front part of a boot to add strength; and thus "vamping" came to mean making the best of anything by helping it out in some way. In music the term is need in reference to supporting a soloist with an extemporized accompaniment, and no doubt the vamp-horns fulfilled a somewhat similar duty for the choirs. But as the statements and conjectures that have been made as to the use of the instruments still in existence in England differ considerably, it will be well to place before the reader all the information on the point that has reached me. According to this, vamp-horns have been used: to call cattle home from the church tower, in the days when lands were unenclosed; to call people from the fields to the services in the church; to summon assistance in time of danger; to give out the psalms and hymns in church; to augment the voice of the Clerk; for one of the singers to sing bass through it; to supply a missing part to the band; to reinforce the voice of the celebrant at High Mass in the middle ages; to enunciate the bass notes without any attempt at pronouncing the words; to give forth the tune before singing; for "Precenting"; for shouting; to rouse labourers in the morning and call them home at night; for a signal to gleaners to begin or leave off work; by the Parish Clerk to announce events (as a crier). An old Sussex Parish Clerk who formerly used the Ashurst vamp-horn stated that he merely sang or shouted down the instrument to make more sound for the singing; and this was most probably the main use to which all the vamp-horns were put to far as the church services were concerned. But their fitness for other more secular purposes would obviously render them liable to be employed in "calling the cattle home" or in bidding the "ploughman homeward plod his weary way."

The shape of the Ashurst example of this quaint instrument is unique; for all of the others are more of the straight trumpet shape, with bell mouths, and only one (the Harrington specimen) is bent in the middle at all. The respective sizes may be of interest:–

Vamp-horn at –	Length		Greatest diameter
	feet	inches	inches
East Leake	7	9	21
Willoughton	6	0	16½
Harrington	5	0	13
Braybrooke	4	0	24
Charing	3	6	16
Ashurst	3	0	7

The FLUTE nearly always figured in the old church bands of Sussex, and it was often used, if no pitch-pipe were available, to sound the note for the choir when the singing was unaccompanied. It was also occasionally employed as a rod for the castigation of small choir-boys

Vamphorn at East Leake, Nottinghamshire

when they misbehaved themselves, thereby enhancing its many virtues in the eyes, or hands, of the choirmaster. The kind of flute that formed so helpful a member of the band was the Transverse or German flute, so-called to distinguish it from the earlier English flute blown from the end. Most of the instruments used in Sussex were of boxwood, about 2ft in length, with only one key. At East Lavant there are two such preserved in the vestry of the Church; one, dated 1821, made by Whitaker & Co., London, was played by Wm. Mitchell (b. 1805. d. 1859); the other, made by Bland & Welter, was the property of Thomas Wackford (b. 1807) and played by him in 1824. The Selsey flute (preserved in a glass case in the Church) was made by D'Almaine and is similar to the Lavant examples.

The small flute or FIFE was not common, perhaps on account of its shrill tone, but two specimens still exist; a small one at Selsey by Clementi & Co. and the other, which I believe was used in the South Bersted Church, (maker A. Martin) now in my possession, is a large one of its kind, without any keys, having for its lowest note g (2nd line in treble stave).

The fife is chiefly associated in our minds to-day with military bands and it has indeed been used in the Army for two centuries, but it has also been employed in various other ways – in Lord Mayors' Shows, in the drama, in the Royal Band and at times when a noise was required to attract a crowd. But its shrill notes were not always popular, and a warrant was issued by Charles II forbidding the playing of fifes without a licence from His Majesty's Sergeant Trumpeter.

As an accompaniment to the Psalms the tone of the fife must have been more distracting than edifying one would imagine; but, as a flautist once pointed out to Charles Hallé in discussing the respective merits of piano and flute, the latter instrument is more portable of the two: and it can at least be said of the fife that it is more portable than the organ.

A great favourite with the old church musicians was the CLARI-ONET a single-reed instrument, of beautiful tone when well played, but capable of dreadful screeches in the hands of an indifferent performer. Probably the choir-boys of former days enjoyed this instrument with mischievous glee when badly played, though it was sometimes used with direful effects for their correction. An old choir-man at Bosham, known throughout the parish in late years as "Grandsire" Arnold, joined the singers at the age of ten years (in 1830) and his seat in the gallery was near the clarionet player. If young Arnold stopped singing for a moment, the bandsman would thrust the bell of his clarionet into the lad's ear and blow a shrill and mighty blast to urge him to renewed effort. The instrument actually used for this edifying purpose is still in existence; it is of boxwood, with only one key left on it. Other Sussex clarionets still extant are at Harting, with 6 keys; a Sidlesham one with 12 keys, probably of about the year 1835 in date; and another of West Tarring made of ivory, with 5 keys.

The clarinet was one of the instruments which that famous old Mid-Sussex "musicianer," John Pennicott played (see frontis illustration of it in his hands). Pennicott led the bands at different times in Amberley, Henfield and Woodmancote Churches.

A grandson of his recently related the following anecdotes of him: Old John Pennicott lived for forty years in one house in Amberley. He was band-master of the church. He was a clarionet player. On one occasion through some misunderstanding with the Vicar, the bands-men, although they attended the Church, refused to play, and the Vicar, who was between 80 and 90 years old asked from the pulpit, "Are you going to play or not?" Pennicott answered for himself and

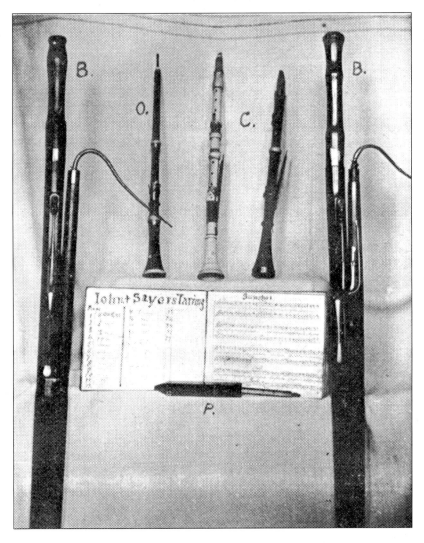

Instruments formerly used in West Tarring Church, Sussex
B. Bassoons.   0. Oboe.   C. Clarionets.   P. Pitchpipe.

his bandsmen, "No!" To which the Parson rejoined, "Well then I'm not going to preach," and forthwith came down out of the pulpit. Later, after the service was over and the Parson walked down the village street, the band came out with their instruments and gave him 'horn-fair' or 'rough music' to the Vicarage. On another occasion, the same band went out on strike. As they would not play at the service of the Church, the Vicar called upon all the inns in the village, and was successful in 'freezing the taps' – that is, the landlords agreed not to serve any of the band with liquor. The bandsmen retorted by whitewashing the Vicar's windows from top to bottom of the house during the night.

The behaviour of the occupiers of the seats in the minstrels' galleries very often indeed lacked that seemliness which one expects in a place of worship, and the voices of both singers and players were frequently uplifted in speech that was neither prayer nor praise. They joined lustily in their share of the service it is true, but if any little incident occurred in the gallery or nave of an unusual nature, they never hesitated to discuss the event in whispers that were by no means inaudible and in language that was not always becoming. One hot summer's day at Bosham a hundred years ago, the leading clarionet-player, warm and sleepy, left out many notes and runs of the music and after a flagging attempt to keep up with the other bandsmen, he laid down his instrument and began mopping his heated brow with a big red handkerchief. The flute-player nudged him and whispered "Play up, will ye!" To which the clarionetist all but shouted a reply that was well heard by all the congregation: "I can't play no more, I do sweats that bad I can't see!"

The Sussex poet Drayton, in his *Polyolbion* mentions the 'shrillest shawn,' which is closely akin to the HAUTBOY or OBOE, a double-reed instrument of penetrating tone, but of lower pitch than the shawm. The oboe was not very commonly played in church bands, but several old specimens are still in existence. The one formerly used at Sidlesham is in my own collection; this is of boxwood, with ivory rings at the joints, and having two keys. Another belonging to Mr. Thomas Holland, West Tarring, a three-keyed oboe, bears the initials T.E. and the date 1791 engraved on two of the keys. There was no nick-name for the oboe in Sussex, but in Dorsetshire it was known as the "Vox Humana."

The oboe is really a *treble shawn*, and the low-toned instrument of the same family called the BASSOON is a *bass shawn*. This is also known as the Fagotto (English *fagot*) from its resemblance to a bundle of sticks, though the old Sussex 'musickers' with whom it was apparently a great favourite, nick-named it the 'horse's leg.' It is a double-reed instrument formed of two wooden pipes joined together at one end, with a curved metal tube at one side on which the reed mouthpiece is placed. The tone of it has been aptly described as 'comic and rustic' and probably the juvenile members of the congregations of old greatly enjoyed the asinine sounds that bad players on the bassoon must have frequently produced. The humorous element in it has been appreciated by composers, for when played in octaves (as in Beethoven's *8th Symphony*) the bassoon can be made to imitate a donkey braying quite successfully. Mendelssohn recognised this when he wrote the music to *Midsummer Night's Dream*, for he employs it in the Overture to suggest the braying of Bottom,

Though hard to play well, on account of the difficulty of keeping perfect tune with it, the bassoon was quite common in the Sussex churches, and several of the bands had two or even more of them; and if tradition be correct Brightling Church (as related before) was the happy possessor of nine bassoons in its band !

At East Ferring the bassoon was played by Mr. Charles Street (born 1770, died 1868), whose daughter, Miss Sarah Street, now in her 91st year, still possesses the instrument, which has 6 keys. Mr. Street generally stuffed some wool into the open end of his bassoon to soften the tone a little. The boys of the village nick-named it "Father's Gun," from the way in which it was carried.

A West Tarring specimen, with 8 keys, now in the possession of Mr. Edward Sayers (author of *Transcripts and Records of the Past: West Tarring*) bears the maker's name 'W. Milhouse, London.' He appears in a London directory for 1808 as "musical instrument manufacturer to the Dukes of Kent and Cumberland"; and this probably fixes the date of this bassoon as the beginning of last century. Another one of West Tarring has 6 keys; a Sidlesham example (in my possession) has,

John Wells, of Lindfield, Born 1812, Died 1856
Original silhouette in possession of Miss Wells

or had, 8 keys; and the bassoon which was played by Mr. John Wells at Lindfield in 1837 has nine keys. Mr. Wells was Sexton and Clerk of Lindfield and was a great musical enthusiast; he died in 1856. His father was Parish Clerk before him, and in following the custom of his day, he would give out a hymn thus: "Let us sing to the praise and glory of God, Hymn 50: tune Hahn'over."

At Heathfield the blacksmith played a bassoon which he called a *Sacbut*.

An instrument that is now practically obsolete in England but still to be met with in France, the SERPENT, was a member of the Selsey, Heathfield, Mayfield and Upper Beeding bands, and probably of others as well. Its name owes its origin to its peculiar shape; this may be seen in the illustration of the Beeding example, which is still extant and preserved in the quaint Museum at Bramber. Invented at the end of the 16th century the Serpent was early adopted for ecclesiastical purposes, being used in France under the name of Serpent d'Eglise to support the plain-chant. Some of the English clergy objected to itg use in Divine worship on the ground that it was unscriptural, but it was not uncommonly employed in England to support the choirs early last century. The Beeding instrument, like others of its kind, is of thin wood, covered with leather, with four keys; and its total length is 7ft. 10in.

Performers on the serpent generally found it difficult to produce the notes accurately and equally in pitch and tone, and in consequence a simpler form of it, with many more keys, was invented early in the 19th century and called the BASS-HORN. Only one church in Sussex, as far as I have been able to discover, used this instrument, and that was at Heathfield. In *Heathfield Memorials* by Percival Lucas, 1910, it is stated: "Four instruments that used to be played in the muscians' gallery are extant – 2 bassoons, 1 bass-horn, and 1 brass serpent in case. They wera some time in posseasion of the Covell family, having become the property of a Mr. Covell, who was Parish Clerk for 30 years." I endeavoured to find these instruments during a visit to Heathfield in 1920, but unfortunately Mr. Covell was then dead and his widow did not know what had become of them. The serpent is described by Mr. Lucas as of brass, but Mr. G. E. Collins,

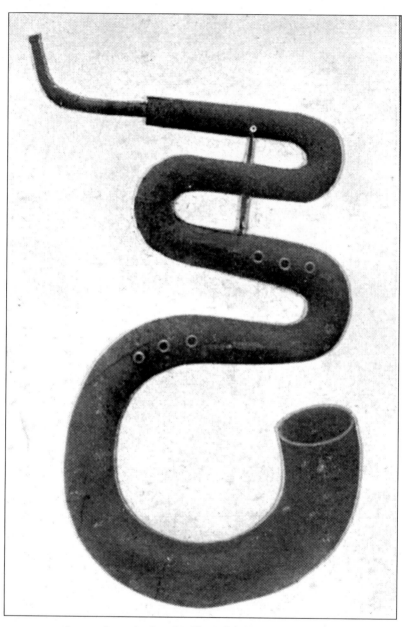

Serpent formerly played in Upper Beeding Church, Sussex

of Waldron Street, Cross-in-hand, informed me in 1917 that his father at one time "played an old wooden instrument in Heathfield Church called the Serpent." The latter statement is probably correct.

The Heathfield band as represented by Mr. Lucas was apparently composed of nothing but bass instruments, but I have ascertained that a flute and clarionet were also used there.

Of the brass wind instruments the two most frequently played in Sussex churches were the CORNET and TROMBONE, both of which are so well known that no description of them is necessary. About 1856 the Psalm-singing at Birdham Church was accompanied by what may be called a "transitional" band, consisting of Cornet, Violin and Harmonium – truly a curious combination.

Generally speaking the advent of a harmonium or organ meant the immediate dissolution of the old band, but here we have two of the band's instruments surviving along with the keyed interloper.

At Westhampnett the cornet was played by a dwarf named Charles Norkett, who stood on a stool while playing. He was a well-known character in the neighbourhood and in spite of his diminutive stature was an enthusiastic cricketer, In an obituary notice of him in the *West Sussex Gazette* it is stated that "Norkett was only 3ft. 4in. high, and that he was formerly a member of Westhampnett Church Choir and played the cornet, or some other instrument when church music was of a more elaborate if less pleasing nature than at present." He died suddenly, aged 61, in 1888, while looking on at a cricket match at Goodwood.

For some time after the Restoration in 1660 there was a dearth of boys' voices, and the clergy supplied the want by introducing cornets, or more properly cornetts, into their churches (Hawkins, *History of Music.*) These were not cornets like the modern brass instrument, but were curved horns of wood covered with leather, with finger-holes in the side. I have not discovered a Sussex example,

An early form of the cornet (about 1820) was called the CORNOPEAN, which had only two pistons.

A young farmer at Berwick (Sussex) was a regular attendant in the middle of the last century, at the church services, for his cornopean and a harmonium (another case of a "transitional band") supplied all the music of that church for some years. It is said that the two instruments "went beautifully together" – but probably distance would have enhanced the beauty.

A few years ago a dear old lady at Henfield, then in her 91st year, gave me some information about the church band and on referring to the clever playing of Pennicott on the TROMBONE, she exclaimed: "What a lot of that brass he could get into his mouth, to be sure!" As a child she had watched him drawing in the long brass crook of the instrument and imagined that he swallowed the crook each time! The trombone was used in several bands, generally where a large number of other instruments were also employed.

At Hailsham early last century a FRENCH-HORN was used in conjunction with a bassoon and clarionet. This was the only place where the French-horn formed part of a Sussex band, as far as I am aware, and its rarity was probably due to the difficulty of playing it with any degree of skill.

As one might expect nearly all the bands had one or more VIOLINS in them, and probably many of these actual instruments still exist, though I have only succeeded in finding a few of them. Unlike the old clarionets, oboes, bassoons and serpents, which all gradually became almost obsolete as far as amateur players were concerned, the fiddle has always maintained its position as a fashionable instrument with everybody. Consequently many violins were preserved and carried off by children or friends of the church minstrels, when no longer required in the churches, while other instruments were allowed to decay or were thrown away. The leaders of the bands usually played the violin or flute, and both instruments provided a ready means of correcting naughty choir-boys, the fiddle-stick or flute itself forming an excellent rod for chastisement.

The violin formerly played by Mr. Coppard (b.1802, d.1872) at Lindfield is still in the possession of his daughter-in-law, Mrs. Coppard, at Brighton, who is in her 92nd year as far as actual age is reckoned, but is still only young in mind and activity. This violin has a short neck with frets on it like those on the neck of a guitar, an unknown addition to most fiddles.

I have not yet unearthed a Viola in Sussex, or ever heard of one as

46

having been played in a Sussex church, though it was used in Dorset; but nearly every band had the next member of the viol family the VIOLONCELLO, or BASS-VIOL as it was generally called. The bass-viol was an earlier form of the violoncello, with more sloping shoulders and a flat back, and consequently with a softer tone than its successor had. It was this soft tone of the old viols that caused them to be ousted by the more brilliant violins and richer-boned 'cellos from the orchestras of Europe, England being the last country to give them up.

One of the 'cellos still in existence is that which was used in Bosham Church, an interesting specimen inasmuch as it is made of thin copper. This instrument was in the possession of the Martin family at Bosham until 1916 when it was sold out of the parish, and, after passing through various hands, found its final resting place in the Boston Museum of Fine Arts, U.S.A. Among the old documents and papers preserved in the parish chest in Bosham Church is a notice that was once posted on the door, containing a quaint reference to the bass-viol, or "bass-voil" as it is spelt:–

"Whereas some evil-disposed person or persons did last evening during the usual time of ringing the Church bells enter the Sacred Edifice and wantonly and maliciously destroy three of the principal strings of the bass-voil in the gallery: Whoever will give information to the Church Wardens so as to lead to the conviction of the Offender or Offenders of such sacriligious conduct, the informers thereof will meet with a satisfactory Reward from certain respective Parishioners who feel themselves interested in the especial care and welfare, and will, if possible, protect from insult, or degradation, an old venerable Church, obviously known to be the most ancient and renowned in the Diocese.

Henry Brooker, Church Warden.
Parish of Bosham,
February 25th, 1844."

Eastbourne is stated to have possessed a copper bass-viol as well as Bosham, but I have been unable to trace the history of this instrument.

Mr. G. Roberts, of Henfield, possesses a home-made 'cello which was formerly used in Shermanbury Church, where Mr. Roberts' father led the band and choir.

Another 'cello still surviving belongs to Mr. Herbert Blackman (Hastings) who purchased it many years ago from an old man named Peter Carey, who played it in Hooe Church.

Angmering once had a musical Rector for 61 years in the person of the Rev. Wm. Kinleside, whose incumbency lasted from 1776 to 1836. He played the 'cello himself and encouraged his church band in every way. Often he drove in his chariot, a ponderous old coach with a pair of sleek horses, to Chichester to attend the concerts held there; and when we know that the Sussex roads were most notoriously bad a century ago, and that the coach probably took at least 2¹/₂ hours to do the 15 miles journey from Angmering to Chichester, we must indeed admire the musical enthusiasm of the worthy Mr. Kinleside.

At Billingshurst there passed away in 1918, in her 82nd year, Mrs. Ireland, daughter of Rev. Henry Beath, Vicar of Billingshurst, 1832-1858. Mrs. Ireland remembered the church band quite well, and often related an amusing instance of childlike imagination on her part. It was impressed upon her when a child that the church was God's House wherein He dwelt, but for a long time it was a mystery to her as to which part of His house one should look in order to see him. At length an extra effort on the part of the player of the bass-viol solved the mystery for her; she came home and said; "I know where God is now; He is inside the big fiddle!"

The DOUBLE-BASS was used in a few of the Sussex churches, and was appropriately and locally known as the "Grandmother Fiddle." The old "musicker" always alluded to the double-bass in the feminine gender, just as church bell-ringers refer to the bells to this day; it is a belfry crime to speak of a bell as "he" or "it." The double-bass is still a true member of the *viol* family, being frequently made with the flat back and sloping shoulders of that class of instruments, of which indeed it is the only survival in actual use for modern music.

Of the stringed instruments that were *plucked*, either with a quill or other plectrum, or by the fingers, very few were apparently used in churches at any time. They were not very suitable for the purpose owing to their inability to sustain a note for any length of time. In the

48

middle ages there were many varieties of plucked instruments in vogue – the Rote, Gittern, Cittole, Pandore, Mandore, Lute, Theorboe, Psaltery, Harp – but their ecclesiastical use seems to have been chiefly confined to sculptured representations of them in the stonework of cathedrals and churches. They were not entirely rejected, however, from use in the services, for in John Playford's *Introduction to the Skill of Music*, 1674, among the Rules for singing the Psalms a reference is made to the Tunes 'as proper to sing to the Organ, Theorbo, or Bass-viol.' The theorbo was a large lute (a tenor-lute) – a plucked instrument.

In Allison's *Psalms* (see later) there is a reference to the lute, orpharion and citterne, but they were probably rarely used in churches. In Sussex the only instrument of this class that was ever used ecclesiastically, as far as I have been informed, was the BANJO, the most modern of its type. The banjo has a more powerful and penetrating tone than the old instruments, but it cannot sustain the sound any longer than they could; and its use in Brightling Church was in all likelihood a matter of expediency, either to pacify some ambitious performer, or to obtain the attendance of some young man at the "prayers-going."

Even the HARP, with its rich tone and extensive compass, was not introduced into any church of Sussex, though the organist at Lindfield about the middle of last century trained his choristers in his own house to the accompaniment of a harp. The-choir-practices were held in his house because the boys "would have been frightened to go and practise in the church at night, with the owls and the bats flying about."

Of the instruments of percussion the DRUM, KETTLE-DRUM and TRIANGLE were all used, but with sufficient rarity to emphasize their unfitness for church services. From time immemorial drums, or tom-toms, have played an important part in the religious ceremonies of nearly all primitive peoples (except in Europe); it has been reserved for Christians and Mohammedans to oust them from public worships. The reason is that rhythm rather than tune satisfies the musical needs of uncultured man, while highly developed minds require melody and harmony as well as rhythm. Neither the old Plainsong, nor the more modern chant and hymn-tune, lends itself to the regular beat of a drum, and only one Sussex church, that at Nuthurst, had such an instrument for use at the services.

Drums were, however, no doubt frequently employed by the bands who played at the "Church Ales." These were popular social meetings, held as a means of making money for the use of the sanctuary and for providing for the poor. The ale was home-brewed, often by the parson himself, itnd frequently sold for the benefit of both clergy and church, as well as the poor. In the Churchwarden's Account-book of West Tarring occurs this entry:–

"1561   It. [item] to the Drowme pleyr   xii d.
It. to the mynssterylls   vi s. viii d.

This was no doubt a payment made to the band at the Church Ale, and apparently the drowme pleyr (drum player) was of such importance that his emolument was entered separately from that of the other minstrels. Perhaps these bands performed inside the churches as well as at the social gathering, but I have not found an instance of this in Sussex.

An old man at Lodsworth informed me some years ago that a KETTLE-DRUM was used in the church there, but I think it most probable that it was a SIDE-DRUM or Snare Drum (such as is used in the military drum and fife bands). A kettle-drum is a large instrument and two or more of them are required in orchestras; and it is scarcely likely that a small village church would have been supplied with one.

As a symbol of the Holy Trinity the TRIANGLE has been known from the earliest Christian days, and the simple little percussion instrument bearing that name has found its way into various places of worship. In the Coptic churches of Old Cairo cymbals, small bells*

---

* In the Armenian Church in Constantinople no musical instruments are used at all, but when the service is engaged in *praise*, a jingling noise is kept up with a quaint implement, called a *Snza*, This consists of a large metal disc at the end of a pole, with a number of small bells hung round it. Two Snzas are continuously rattled until the service reverts to prayer or preaching.

and triangles were all employed in the accompaniment of the hymns in the middle of the 19th century; and in 1846 a Triangle formed part of the Rustington church band. The sounds produced by a triangle are not of a very dignified or solemn character; but neither were many of the "interludes" played between the verses of some of the old Psalm-tunes (see the example in Chap. iii.) and the bright little jingler was quite worthy of much of the music of the period.*

Several kinds of keyed or keyboard wind instruments found a place in Divine worship during the Past before the arrival of the harmonium and American organ. At Albourne, some 60 or 70 years ago, a man named Grinstead played a FLUTINA, a kind of a cross between an accordion and a concertina. He stood behind the "winch-organ" to play, and quite possibly his performance was of the nature of a vamping accompaniment, without a music-book.

Another of the same class was a SERAPHINE, the immediate precursor of the harmonium. The seraphine was invented by John Green, of Soho Square, London, in 1833, and consisted of a set of "free reeds" enclosed in a case, with keyboard and bellows. The tone is described as harsh and raspy, and incapable of expression, in Grove's *Dictionary of Music*. This description of it does not tally, however, with the account given by Mr. W. Frost, of Cocking, who stated in 1917 in a letter, that "It was very much like a large box, and played as a harmonium, having a short keyboard, and blown by a lever on the right-hand side. Could be blown by foot or hand. No stops, quite a pleasant and soft tone, but rather monotonous. I think it would have been about 4ft. long, 2ft. wide and 3ft high. It was in Cocking Church about 1885. It was afterwards used in the School, but what became of it I cannot find out, and I left the parish about that time for a considerable period. The pipes were entirely closed in, some metal ones, upright in the front part, and the Bass, etc., wooden ones piled one over another horizontally at the back, with a large bellows underneath." In a sketch in his letter Mr. Frost shows that the

---

* A barrel-organ that once stood in a Church in Gloucestershire, now in the possession of Mr. W. H. Hickox, Kensington, has five stops: Diapason, Principal, Fifteenth, *Drum* and *Triangle*.

Cocking instrument had a compass of 3½ octaves.

As will be seen from this description the seraphine at Cocking was not a free-reed instrument but really a small pipe-organ. It is possible, however, that the pipes were only dummy ones for ornamental show, such as are often placed on American organs for that purpose.

Cocking is the only place in Sussex that had a seraphine as far as I know, but probably other churches also had them, for the inventor of it pushed his musical contrivance with great vigour and sold many specimen all over the country. In Sussex the name seraphine, or seraphim, was sometimes erroneously applied to the barrel-organ.

At Balcombe, during the inter-regnum between the dissolution of the band and the advent of the organ, a CONCERTINA provided the musical accompaniment of the Psalm-singing. To many people the concertina is solely associated with the Cockney holiday-maker and his vocal efforts, and the idea of its presence in a church may seem to border on the sacrilegious; but a good player with a first-class concertina can obtain some brilliant effects and put a great amount of expression into them as well. Apart from its secular associations it is really no more inappropriate to the sanctuary than is a strident harmonium. And the concertina has at least the merit of being a little more antique* than the harmonium – a commendable virtue in ecclesiastical matters!

In most of the churches of Sussex where no band was available, or where a band had ceased to exist or not yet come into being, the accompaniments to the Psalms were nearly always provided by a BARREL-ORGAN, an instrument that had the obvious advantage over all others that it could be played withouilearning or practice – the performer simply turned a handle and pumped the bellows or "feeders."

These organs were in great vogue for about a hundred years, and were in various sizes, some having several stops and others none. They were generally furnished with three separate "barrels," each having ten or twelve tunes which could be brought into action as

---

* The concertina was patented by Wheatstone in England in 1829; the harmonium by Debain in France in 1840.

required. The barrels were wooden cylinders about 3ft. 6in. long and 8 or 9 inches in diameter, with pins or staples on them varying in length according to the duration of the notes. These staples raised certain keys and thus worked the mechanism that allowed the wind to reach the required pipes. The barrel-organs used in churches rarely had complete chromatic scales of notes, but only enough pipes to form the two or three major scales of G and D, or G, D and A ; and all the tunes marked on the barrels had to be transposed into one or other of those keys. One result of this was that whenever a "winch-organ" as the barrel-organ was called, was converted into a "finger-organ" (a key-board one) which was frequently done, all the music played thereon had to be in one or other of the keys of the original instrument, or be transposed accordingly, unless the missing pipes were added.

An interesting letter on this subject was sent to me in 1917 by the late Mr. A. W. Lambert, of Chichester, who had at one time been organist of Singleton. He wrote: "It was in 1870 when I was first articled to Dr. Gladstone [then organist of Chichester Cathedral] the Schoolmaster turned it [the barrel-organ] into a Manual Organ, but it could only be played in three keys, D, A and E. We had to arrange all the music in those three keys. I well remember on the occasion of Bishop Gilbert's death I was asked to play the *Dead March*, and I had to play it in the key of A, If I remember rightly there were only four octaves. I cannot remember the number of barrels but I believe there were three. The blowing was done by a boy turning the handle, I think it was sold to Mr. Dean, of North Street."

There are only two barrel-organs now in existence in Sussex churches, one at Brightiing and the other at Piddinghoe; but only the former is still "on active service," the latter having been put out of action long ago.

The Brightling example was given to the Church by the renowned John Fuller who was "borned" in 1757 and died in 1834, He was an M.P. for Sussex and had two excellent hobbies to direct; his mind from politics – science and music. When the organ was given, Fuller presented the male members of the choir with white smocks, buckskin breeches and yellow stockings, and the girls with red cloaks, to be used during the service on the day the organ was first played and afterwards. This winch-organ has 43 notes, and seven stops: Open Diapason, Stopped Diapason, Principal, Octave Flute, 15th, Mixture and one other (name label gone). There are two barrels, each with twelve tunes (including *Old 100th*, *Christians Awake*, and *Jesus Christ is risen to-day*) most of them having many "repeats and twiddles" in them in the way of runs and shakes. The organ is in a gallery at the west end of the church, and the performer stands behind it and blows with his left foot on a pedal, while his hands are occupied in "grinding" the handle and manipulating the stops. The tone of the instrument is good and powerful. At present it is used only for ingoing and concluding voluntaries, the singing in the services being accompanied by a modern Positive organ in the nave.

The Piddinghoe instrument is very dilapidated and unplayable, having been stored away in a barn for many years. It has 2 barrels with 10 tunes; 28 notes; 3 stops – Open Diapason, Principal and Fifteenth.

There are at Hartfield Church in the belfry, the remains of an old barrel-organ, which is stated to have been made by Bryceson and installed in the Church in 1726, but the date of it is probably later. It is now beyond repair and much out of order.

In the long gallery of the house at Parham Park, there is preserved the barrel-organ which was formerly used in Parham Church. The instrument is about 6ft. high by 8ft 6in wide, and it has four barrels (one missing), three with secular tunes and one with 9 Psalm tunes and the *Easter Hymn*. There are four stops, all un-named, but judging from the pipes they are probably Open Diapason, Stopped Diapason, Dulciana and Principal; there are 24 pipes (24 notes) to each stop. The organ was removed from the Church, some fifty years ago or so, to make way for a harmomium, much to the regret of the late Lord Zouche (of Parham) who thought it much nicer than the new instrument; for on the barrel-organ there were only ten tunes and you knew what to expect!

The barrel-organ is un-dated, but judging from its secular tunes, it was made between 1790 and 1800. One of the latter is a song entitled *He's ay a Kissing me*, and another is, *With my mug in my hand*. It is to be hoped that the Parish Clerk did not put these on instead of the *Old 100th* at any time.

Barrel-organ in Brightling Church, Sussex
(From photo by T. Croft in "The Annals of Brightling Church" by W. F. Cooper.)

Many of the old barrel-organs had secular tunes as well as sacred melodies, and very often they were used to entertain the bucolic (and alcoholic) peasant mind in the village inn. This mingling of the celestial music with the worldy, the spiritual with the spirituous, led to unhallowed results sometimes. The barrel-organ in Berwick (Sussex) Church had clockwork for its motive-power, and on one occasion instead of stopping at the end of a Psalm the mechanism gave a "click," and the congregation were then regaled with a comic song entitled *Little Drops of Brandy*; after which there was another 'click' and then – *Go to the Devil and wash yourself!*"

About 1830 Jevington resolved to have a winch-organ and a farmer Churchwarden was deputed to fetch it in his waggon from London. At the same time his spouse, bent on being cleanly as well as Godly, commissioned him to bring her a new washing-machine. Both were duly brought down from "Lunnon" on a Saturday; but driving teams on dusty roads was thirsty work, and turnpike inns were open-doored and enticing: so the sacred organ was deposited in the farm house kitchen and the mundane washer was set down in the Church!

At Stanmer the barrel-organ also had a key-board, and – "the organ was played by the honorable Ladies at the mansion; when they left home we fell back on the wretched barrel. This had many evils; it could not be lightly suppressed when once its services were employed. Occasionally we had an instrumental solo after the words were finished, but we were never so badly fixed as the good folks at Wannock were reputed to have been. We could not have carried our persistent barrel out of Church, if we had been so minded. Their barrel could not be silenced even when thrown into an open grave, for tradition says that it then began on its own – *All people that on earth below*."

The earliest barrel-organ in Sussex, as far as my records go, was that of Hartfield Church, if the date of it is correctly given in C. N. Sutton's *History of Hartfield*, but as stated above the date (1726) is probably wrong. Rye obtained one in 1811, Salehurst in 1836, East Ferring about 1870, Angmering in 1852. Steyning had its winch-organ transformed into a finger-organ in 1853, but the barrels were still left in the interior of the instrument up to 1894, when the present three-manual organ was installed in its place.

At Rogate there are some remains of a barrel in the village; and at Harting the Rector possesses the box in which the spare barrels were formerly kept.

The following advertisement appeared in the *West Sussex Gazette* on June 25th, 1857 – quaint reading in the present days:–

"Church Organ. For sale an excellent barrel-organ in wainscote case with gilt; pipes in front. It has 3 barrels each playing 10 Psalm-tunes. The above instrument was made by Bryceson, has 4 stops and will be sold for the very moderate price of 8 guineas. Apply Mr. Bennett, North Street, Cbichester."

The *Musical Times* in 1860 had two advertisements in its columns: one of "a perfect gem of a Finger-Organ, 4¹/₂ octaves, containing 4 stops"; the other of a "Barrel-Organ playing 40 Psalm-tunes and chants, four barrels." These two announcements indicate the transitional period between the two kinds of organs.

About 60 or 70 years ago an old man named Fleming made an organ for the church at Burwash and this was the only instrument there for many years. In course of time both the organ and its maker became old and decrepit, and the parish earnestly longed to get rid of the wheezy instrument; but it would have broken the old man's heart to have suggested its abolition, and the parishioners had to endure it patiently until Fleming's decease enabled them to free themselves from what had become an instrument of torture.

Two pathetic anecdotes may fitly close the story of Sussex barrel-organs. The first is from the reminiscences of Mr. Edward Sayers:–

"I believe the wooden parts of the organ [of West Tarring Church] came into the possession of my great-grandfather, John Lindup, a cooper, at West Tarring. He left his business, by will, to my father who made all kinds of wooden utensils for household, dairy, brewery use, etc., and I remember, when very young, seeing him, when he wanted a piece of well-seasoned wood, cut off a piece of the 'Organic remains' which consisted of a large mahogany front on which the royal arms were painted and some large wooden square pipes."

The second is from the recollections of Mr. Fred Jones, of East Hoathly:–

"In my present home we had a clever clocksmith, an original character who bought a church barrel-organ which took up the greater part of his parlour. This was a rare treasure and often shown to the stranger. A gentleman from college, reputed to be a skilful organist, inspected my friend's treasure and immediately put his foot in it by declaring it was out of tune. He offered to correct the defects and a few days after began to cut down and hack the pipes (diabolical sacrilege!). After working his own sweet will for a time he gave up the experiment. My poor old friend was in despair, but he set to work and in three months he had soldered on all the treasured pieces that had been hacked off."

In the churches where neither band nor barrel-organ was available the singing was rendered without any accompaniment, the key-note of the tune being given out on a PITCH-PIPE by the Parish Clerk. These pipes were made of wood, about 18 or 19 inches in length, and in section about 1½in square. The mouth-piece, at one end, was similar to that of an ordinary tin-whistle, while at the other end was a wooden plug on which the notes of the scale were marked. The plug was pulled out to the indication mark of the required note, the pipe was then blown, and the members of the choir took their own particular note by singing the word "Praise!," or "Praise ye the Lord!" When all had obtained their proper notes, the leader gave a signal and off they started on what must have often been an uncertain musical venture.

Bosham pitch-pipe
Sketched by Henry Henshall, R.W.S.

Several of the old pitch-pipes are still in existence, and those of Bosham (discovered by myself among a pile of rubbish in the 13th century oak chest in the church), Brede and East Lavant are fortunately preserved in their respective churches. The Ditchling and

Selmeston pitch-pipes are in my own possession,

Mr. Thomas Hyde, of Worthing, has an interesting specimen inasmuch as it is *round*, not square, in section (length 12in., diameter 1³/₄in.) This, he believes, was formerly used in Broadwater Church.

Here is a reminiscence of Mr. James Miles, of Worthing: "When I was about 10 years old [in 1848] I played the Violin in Findon Church, the three other musicians were the School-master, Bass-Viol; Harry Goodger (the Vicar's gardener) Clarionet; and Mr. Marsh (Head Gardener to Lady Bath at Mundham) Flute. A Pitch-pipe was also used by me, which I set to the first note of the hymns, to start the singers, but the plug of the pipe sometimes, unfortunately, got pushed in just before I blew it, and I shall never forget the discordant noise, nor the, to me, awful sounds usually produced by the instruments."

The pitch-pipe was sometimes called a spoke-pipe in Sussex.

In 1599 a musician named Richard Allison published a collection of the Psalms entitled, *The Psalmes of David in meter, the plaine song beinge the common tune to be sung and plaide upon the lute, orpharion, citterne, or base violl, severally or altogether, the singing part to be either tenor or treble to the instrument, according to the nature of the voyce, etc.* From this it would appear that other instruments besides the organ were used for accompanying the Psalms before 1660; but Allison's collection was intended chiefly for private use, and the four parts of the music were so printed on each page that four persons sitting round a table could sing out of the same book. It is probable, however, that the collection was used in a few churches and possibly to the accompaniment of some of the instruments mentioned in the title. These were all stringed instruments – the lute, orpharion and citterne being held and played in practically the same manner as the guitar, while the bass-violl, or bass-viol, was the forefather of the violoncello.

There is no direct evidence, however, that Allison's book was used in any church, or that the instruments named in its title-page were played and there is no doubt that down to the middle of the 17th century the Organ was practically the only instrument in general use in our churches; but it does not quite come within the scope of this book; for it was almost entirely ousted during the period under consideration. A brief reference, however, to the King of Instruments may be of interest. Rye Church had several organs in former days; one in the choir and a larger one in the transept.

In Rye Churchwardens' Accounts appears this item under the date 1513:–

	£	s	d
"for the bringing the organ from London to Rye	1	3	8

In 1514:–

"For scouring and mending the old organ nowstanding in Our Lady Chapel 10   0

In 1523:–

"Pd. the organ maker; for making St. George's organ   1   4

The last item was probably for repairs or tuning and could not have been for actual manufacture.

In the West Tarring Churchwardens' Accounts (transcribed by Edward Sayers) occurs:–

"1570 B. [received] for Orgayne Pypes   Xs."

Rotherfield Accounts contain these items:–

"1532 May 19. And for the old organs   Xd."
"1606 Aug. 3. Oertaine orgle pipes."

I have been unable to discover any reference to the organ as existing in Sussex churches during the latter half of the 17th and the whole of the 18th Centuries; it is not till the middle of the 19th Century that it reappears. There can be no doubt that in some respects, chiefly perhaps in the matter of correctness of pitch and tune, the re-introduction of the organ was an advantage; but it was in one way a disaster: for with the arrival of the Organ, the Harmonium and its feeble sister the American Organ, all the old "musicianers" and lusty singers, with their boundless enthusiasm and fervent diligence, their homely piety and simple sincerity, disappeared from our churches, perhaps for ever.

Charles Street, of Ferring, Sussex. Born 1790, Died 1868

THE MUSIC

The musical outlook of our forefathers in the Past; was evidently a limited one, for the energies of both composers and performers seem to have been chiefly confined to the music of the metrical versions of the Psalms, and of a few anthems and hymns. This remark refers mainly, of course, to the church musicians of Sussex in the 18th and early part of the 19th Centuries, but it also applies largely to those of England generally during the same period.

The composition of metrical versions of Holy Scripture was a common employment of ecclesiastics during the middle ages; and the custom is stated to have arisen in imitation of the old Teutonic chronicles of domestic and national transactions which were recorded in metre. The Saxon and Waldensian clergy composed these metrical paraphrases in order to assist the memory; or to provide the secluded monk or wandering pilgrim with some hallowed strain as a solace in his loneliness; or to supply the minstrel with some more worthy theme than the faery legend or the gay romaunt. Most of these compositions were designed only for private or secular use; they were not used in the service of the Church till the Reformation, when they were adopted for the benefit of the congregations, who were now to take part in the singing for the first time since the earliest days of Christianity. For about two or three centuries after the Apostolic age all the singing at the services was congregational, but a special order of singers (*Psalmistæ*) began to arise about the beginning of the 4th century to whom alone was committed the rendering of psalms and hymns. These "canonical singers" were mentioned at the Council of Laodicea (about A.D. 363).

With the dawn of the Reformation, however, the primitive custom of congregational singing was revived and the disciples of Wickcliffe sang metrical psalms in the 14th century; and in the next century John Huss, in Germany, versified the 128th Psalm and introduced metrical psalmody, with music of slow notes of equal length.

The metrical psalms were never an essential part of the Prayer-

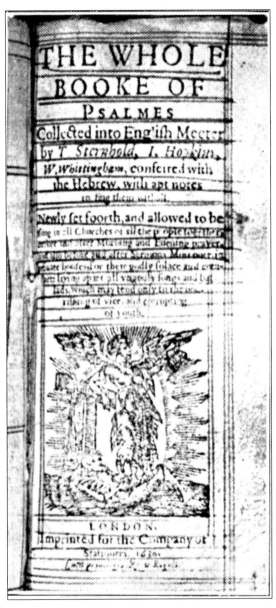

Title page of Old Version with tunes
in possession of Mr. E. Collins, Bramber

book Services, but were used at certain intervals without disturbing the rest of the service. This use was based on the injunction of Queen Elizabeth, that "in the beginning or the end of Common Prayer there may be sung an hymn or such-like song to the praise of Almighty God in the best sort of melody or music that may be conveniently devised, having respect that the sense of the hymn may be understood and perceived."

Of the numerous early metrical versions of the psalms in English that by Sternhold and Hopkins and others, issued for the first time with about 40 tunes in 1562, was practically everywhere the most popular. This was the "Old Version" as distinguished from the "New Version" of Tate and Brady, published in 1696. It is stated by J. Holland in *The Psalmists of Great Britain* (1843) that the Psalms in whole or in part, had been rendered into English verse by over 150 authors; of which about 70 were complete versions, amongst them being one by Dr. King, Bishop of Chichester, 1642-1669.

The Old Version owed its origin to Thomas Sternhold, Groom of the Robes to Henry VIII, who translated and published 51 psalms in 1549. To these were added later 58 others by John Hopkins, a Schoolmaster; five more by a Priest named William Whittyngham, and others by Thomas Newton, a Barrister, Robert Wisdome, and by a Scotch divine named William Keshe. The whole of these were collected together and published, with music, in 1562 by John Day; and the work was for a long time commonly known as *Day's Psalter.* It is worth noting that the first two versifiers of the Psalms in English were laymen, and it is their names that have survived while the others associated with them are all but unknown.

In Sussex the Old Version and the New Version of Tate and Brady (1696) superseded nearly all the others.

The language of these two Versions is simple, direct and easy to be understood – obvious causes of their popularity. Moreover the words jingle along, like Scott's poetry, in strongly marked rhythm, and they can be more readily committed to memory than can many poems of much greater merit. A comparison of three versions of the 1st Psalm, of which the third is by far the best poetry, will exemplify this statement:–

OLD VERSION

1. The man is blest that hath not lent
   to wicked men his ear,
Nor led his Life as sinners do
   nor sat in scorner's chair.

2. But in the Law of God the Lord
   doth set his whole Delight:
And in the same doth exercise
   himself both day and night.

3. He shall be like a Tree that is
   planted the Rivers nigh:
Which in due Season bringeth forth
   its Fruit abundantly.

NEW VERSION

1. How blest is he who ne'er consents
   by ill advice to walk;
Nor stand in sinners' ways, nor sita
   where men profanely talk.

2. But makes the perfect law of God
   his business and delight;
Devoutly reads therein by day
   and meditates by night.

3. Like some fair tree, which, fed by streams,
   with timely fruit doth bend,
He still shall nourish, and success
   all his designs attend.

VERSION BY JAMES MERRICK

1. O how blest the man, whose ear
    Impious counsels shuns to hear;
    Who nor loves to tread the way
    Where the Sons of Folly stray,
    Nor their frantic mirth to share,
    Seated in Derision's chair;
    But, to Virtues' path confin'd,
    Spurns the men of sinful mind,

2. And, possessed with sacred awe,
    Meditates, great God, thy law.
    This by day his fix'd employ,
    This by night his constant joy.

3. Like the tree that, taught to grow
    Where the streams irriguous flow,
    Oft as the revolving Sun
    Through the destin'd months has run,
    Regular, its seasons knows,
    Bending low its loaded boughs,
    He his verdant branch shall spread,
    Nor his sick'ning leaves shall shed;
    He, whatever his thoughts devise,
    Joyful to the work applies,
    Sure to find the wish'd success
    Crown his hope, his labour bless.

Another verse or two from the Old Version will afford an idea of the
beauties of the "poetry" in which the pious aspirations of our forefathers were clothed:–

> So many buls do compass me
> That be full strong of head,
> Yea, buls so fat, as though they had
> In Basan field been fed.

They shall heap sorrow on their heads;
Which run as they were mad;
To offer to the idle gods
Alas! it is too bad!

And in Psalm LXXIV, v. 12 the Almighty is addressed in most ludicrous terms:–

"Why doost withdraw Thy hand aback,
And hide it in Thy lappe,
O pluck it out and be not slack
To give Thy toes a rappe."

One can only call such poetry sheer doggerel, and much ridicule and criticism have been aimed at Sternhold and Hopkins for their attempt to make a poetic version of the Psalms. A Cavalier poet, Edward Philips, described some one singing a portion of the Old Version with a woeful noise:–

"Like a cracked saints' bell jarring in the steeple,
Tom Sternhold's wretched prick-song for the people."

When the Earl of Rochester heard the sound of psalm-singing in a church he wrote:–

"Sternhold and Hopkins had great qualms,
When they translated David's Psalms,
To make the heart right glad;
But had it been King David's fate
To hear thee sing and them translate,
By God! 'twould set him mad!"

In spite, however, of the adverse opinion of those with cultured taste, the Old Version became so popular that Bishop Jewel in the 17th century said that he had seen six thousand persons, old and young, assemble round Paul's Cross to sing the Psalms in metre; and there can be no doubt that the people obtained a knowledge of the Psalms through Sternhold and Hopkins such as they would hardly have gained in any other way.

It was often a matter of necessity that the Psalms should be learnt by heart by our ancestors, for many of them were quite illiterate and could neither read nor write. Naturally, therefore, those versions of the Psalms which could be most easily grasped and retained by the simple minds of the untutored "musicianers" were the most popular and the most widely used; and the Old and New Versions were generally deemed to fulfil all the requirements of the old-time choirs in a satisfactory manner.

Many marvellous feats of memory are recorded of unlettered folk in all countries, and those of Sussex people, in the days when most of the villagers "weren't no scholards and never knowed 'ow to read," were quite as wonderful as those of other places.

Reference has already been made to the Horsham singer named Burstow, who could sing 400 songs by heart; and the leader of the choir at Twineham, some 70 or 80 years ago, who sang the whole of the Psalms and many anthems besides from memory.*

The majority of the old compilers of tune-books were fully alive to the popular taste in the matter of words, though they were perhaps not always aware of the reason for it, and as a consequence Sternhold and Hopkins, and Tate and Brady were nearly always the chosen authors of the metrical Psalms to which they set their tunes, while Watts was their favourite hymn-writer.

During the Past there were forty-five different psalmodies and hymn-books that were used in Sussex churches, so far as I have been able to discover, in addition to the innumerable manuscripts written by the musicians themselves. Of the printed books twelve were published by editors who were either natives of, or residents in the County itself; they were generally compiled for some particular church. These indigenous books naturally claim our first attention.

The most noteworthy of them was a splendid volume entitled

---

* When I was in Macedonia in 1918 I heard a Serbian gypsy band play for *four* hours without a note of music in front of them.

Improved Psalmody, compiled by the Rev. William Dechair Tattersall, A.M., Rector of Westbourne, and published in 1794. The words chosen were: "The Psalms of David from a Poetical Version originally written by the Reverend James Merrick, A,M., Fellow of Trinity College, Oxford," while the music was "collected from the most Eminent Composers." The book is bound in leather (oblong, 10³/₄in. by 8¹/₂in) and contains 348 pages of music, beautifully printed from special plates, and 46 pages of introductory letter-press. There is also a List of Subcribers, among whom appear Dr. Dupuis, Guiseppe Haydn, Mus. Doc. Oxon., Samuel Johnson, Esq., and other well-known names. The work opens with a fine dedication to King George III:–

"To the King's Most Excellent Majesty.
Sire,
In aspiring to dedicate to your Majesty a Work, which has for its sole object the service of Religion, and the credit of the National Church, I have only sought to place your name, where every action of your life and reign has tended to establish it, in connection with true piety and public spirit. To doubt, that in the mind of every well-disposed person throughout your Majesty's dominions, the sanction of your name to such a work, will have peculiar weight, would be at once injurious to your Majesty and to your Subjects. With far other sentiments, and with every feeling of loyalty and attachment,
    I am your Majesty's most obedient and devoted Subject,
                      W. D. TATTERSALL."

After this fine address comes an "Advertisement" from which an extract is here given:–

"The late Dr. Thomas, Bishop of Rochester, was equally gratified with the new form given to this version [Merrick's], and recommended it to be sung with the selected tunes by the Choir of bis Church at Bromley. His Lordship, in answer to the first letter of the Editor, returned his thanks for (what he condescended to style) a well-turned application of Mr. Merrick's psalms, to the much "wanted improvement of church music; or rather, to the more sensible and edifying use of it in parochial churches."

As will be seen in this and other quotations from preface or introductions to the old psalmodies, the compilers almost invariably complained of the low state of church music at the time, and expressed their confident hope that their own particular work would effect an improvement in this important part of public worship.

After the Advertisement in Tattersall's book follows an "Address to Dr. Hayes, Dr. Dupuis, Dr. Parsons, Mr. Callcott. Rev. Osborne Wight, Mr. Webbe, Mr. Shield and Mr. Stevens," in which occurs an interesting reference to Haydn, who was then in his 65th year:–

"Dr. Haydn (who may be looked upon as naturalized in this country, from having taken his degree at one of our Universities, and who may perhaps be justly esteemed the most celebrated composer of the present day); Dr. Arnold, Mr. John Stafford Smith, and Mr. Atterbury, having allowed me the honour of reckoning them in the number of my respectable co-adjutors, they will, I trust, excuse my mentioning thus publicly the offer they have now made me of their services, and permit me to assure them, that I am happy to obtain their consent to add their names to my list."

From this it would appear that some of the tunes were specially written for Tattersall's work by the famous composer of *The Creation* himself.

Another part of the Address gives a vivid picture of the state of Church music generally at the end of the 18th century:–

"The performance of psalmody in London is open to many objections. Whatever be the subject of the psalm, the tunes that are chosen are very solemn, and, in most of the parish churches they are rendered still more solemn by the slow manner in which they are usually played. The clerk and the charity children are almost the only performers, and although a person is employed to instruct the young people, nevertheless there seems to be no management in the regulation of their voices. ... The children most commonly rise beyond the natural pitch of their voice, and it becomes rather a general unisonous scream, than either concord, or harmony.

In country parishes, the psalms are chosen, that consist of four parts, and it is thought by the people who form themselves into a choir, that their performance will be very defective, if they do not contrive to fill them all. There are men who travel, and style themselves professors of, and instructors in psalmody; they are furnished with books of their own selections which are seldom correct, and these are disposed of in every place where they go. While such measures are countenanced, it is impossible to expect, that their disciples, should ever arrive at any degree of perfection. The harmony is generally indifferent; but if it were faultless, the counter-tenors are for the most part poorly managed. ...

It was my first object to have published a selection from ancient authors; however since according to your judgment it is easier to provide new tunes, than to adapt those of others for this work, I am willing to follow your advice by rejecting many of them; for, it is a tact, which cannot have escaped general observation, that as the poetry, from the obsoleteness, of the terms and phrases, has not failed to excite ridicule, so the music, from its dulness, or the want of melody has too often produced a contrary effect, *viz.*, that of inviting sleep."

The body of the work consists of selections from Merrick's version of Psalms 1 to 75, set to 217 tunes (an unusually large number for that date) with an Appendix of 28 pages of other tunes. Each page is printed from a special copper-plate and the cost of the production of the volume must have been enormous. The title page states that the Psalms are issued "With New Music," which obviously indicates that the tunes were specially composed or arranged for the work. It is interesting to know that Haydn, amongst others, composed some music for the particular benefit of a Sussex parson! Many well-known names occur in the list of composers of tunes in the book besides that of Haydn, *viz*: Worgan, Webbe, Hayes, Shield, Dupuis, etc. The tunes are written in open score for three parts only, two trebles and a bass, with the idea of bringing the music more within the ability of average choirs than would have been the case if they had been written in four part harmony. The expression marks and terms are quaint and they seem oddly unfamiliar to anyone accustomed to the usual Italian terms, for most of them are in plain and simple English; thus – *loud, soft, chearful, slow, a little quicker, tenderly, lively, loud and with spirit, with energy, chearfull but not too fast or too loud, rather brisk, soothingly.*

Tattersall intended issuing a second volume of his Psalmody, but his object was never accomplished.

Early in the 19th century a Brighton musician, Nathaniel Cooke, organist of the Parish Church, made a remarkable contribution to Sussex church music by issuing *A Collection of Psalms and Hymns, sung at the Parish Church Brighthelmston*, a work that went through three editions. The copy in my possession is the 2nd edition, and this contains 93 tunes (set to the New Version) of which no less than 78 were composed by the assiduous compiler himself. Many of these tunes are of great merit, written in four parts with a certain feeling of dignity and repose not commonly found in similar compositions of the same period. More than half of the tunes are in triple time ($^3/_2$ or $^3/_4$) and a typical example of them is given in facsimile (slightly reduced in size) below.

Facsimile of tune from Nathaniel Cooke's Collection of Psalms and Hymns

Nathaniel Cooke was a true son of Sussex, having been born in Bosham, where he was buried in 1827, His tomb is in the chancel of the Church and the inscription on it is;

Sacred to the memory of Nathaniel Cooke, A Native of this Parish, And many years Organist of Brighton Church. Who died April 5th, 1827, Aged 54 years.

Cooke was faithful to the county of his birth even in his compositions, for he named all his tunes after the towns and villages of Sussex, including all parts of the county and places of all degrees of importance. The list of names will be of some interest to the dwellers in the land of the Downs and Weald, so here are the titles of all the tunes, in the order in which they occur in Cooke's book:–

Chichester, Brighton, Arundel, Steyning, Bosham, Preston, Worthing, Shoreham, Hastings, Cuckfield, Broadwater, Lewes, Newtimber, Alfriston, Newhaven, Portslade, Rottingdean, Poynings, Henfield, Ditchling, Battel, Hailsham, Midhurst, Grinstead, Winchelsea, Uckfield, Southover, Bramber, Waldron, Seaford, Robertsbridge, Crawley, Storrington, Horsham, Hurstperpoint, Chailey, Ovingdean, Southwick, Sompting, Chiddingly, Shermanbury, Birdham, Angmering, Selsea, Tarring, Boxgrove, Lavant, Bolney, Itchenor, Jevington, Prinsted, Worth, Rye, Ewhurst, Fairlight, Mayfield, Selmeston, Crowborough, Finden, Beeding, Dallington, Amberley, Stoke, Ringmer, Newick, Ashburnham, Edburton, Sidlesham, Pulborough, Petworth. (The remaining tunes by Cooke are set to special hymns or canticles and are not named.)

Two other contributions to Sussex church musie were made by Chichester organists, father and son. The earlier work is undated, but it was issued a little before 1815, in which year a former owner of my copy inscribed her name and date: *M. Alcock, March 21st, 1815.* The title of the book is: *Sacred Melodies. A Collection of Psalms and Hymns as sung at the Cathedral Church, and the Chapel of St, John the Evangelist, Chichester, composed, selected, and adapted By T. Bennett, Organist.* Mr. Bennett was organist of the Cathedral from 1817 to 1848, but had acted as deputy from 1803. His book was issued by subscription at 7s. 6d., and in the List of Subscribers appear many names that are familiar in Chichester and the neighbourhood at the present time, e.g. Charge, Caffin, Freeland, Gruggen, Gatehouse, Newland, Woods. There are 32 tunes in the book, written in two parts only (treble and bass), most of them taken from earlier collections, only one, entitled "Sussex" * being by Bennett himself.

A few years later another and enlarged edition of this work was published in six volumes, and it was evidently a popular collection of tunes, for it ultimately reached a 5th edition with 180 tunes in it. In the later issues the compiler made a novel and amusing departure by renaming many of the old familiar tunes after local places, no matter who the composer happened to be. Thus we have 'Littlehampton' by Dr. Croft, 'Cowdray' by Dr. Hayes, 'Lavant' by Battishill, 'Woolbeding' by Gluck, 'Fittleworth' by Mozart, 'Aldwick' by Beethoven, 'Emsworth' by Dr. Arne, 'Graffham' by Pleyel, 'Eartham' by Rousseau, and 'Oving' by Haydn! This latter is an adaption of 'The Heavens are telling' from *The Creation*, The well-known 'Sicilian Mariners' tune is brought into use and called 'Slindon.'

Thomas Bennett left four musical sons to carry on his name and fame, one of whom, Thomas J. Bennett, also compiled a tune-book: *A Selection from the New Version of the Psalms and from the Hymns appended to the Book of Common Prayer, Adapted to Appropriate Tunes, by T. J. Bennett, Organist of St. Paul's, Chichester.* This work is undated but was probably issued about 1850. It contains 51 tunes for Psalms and 4 for hymns. A curious coincidence occurs in these two books by the Bennetts; in each of them is a tune called "Chichester," one by Collick and the other by Marsh, and although they are supposed to be different tunes they both begin and end the melody with 2½ bars almost exactly alike.

Several psalmodies were compiled expressly for particular parishes, a fact which showa how eager were our forefathers to have plenty of singing in the services, for these books were very costly to produce and their circulation could have been only a limited one. In 1842 an anonymous book was published by William Hayley Mason, of Chichester, entitled – *A Collection of Psalms, Hymns, Anthems and Collects as sung at Selsey Church.* The Preface is worth quoting as an example of the ingenuous vanity of the compilers of the olden days:–

---

* *Another tune named "Sussex" appeared in Lock Hymn Tunes, published in London in 1769.*

"It has been compiled from the works of the most pious and approved authors, and, it is hoped, is free from most of the objections which unfortunately attach to many similar collections, via, of being deficient in metrical harmony and arrangement, poor in expression, and frequently not exempt from doctrinal error. Thus an opportunity is now afforded to every member of the Congregation of joining in a portion of the service which has been hitherto grievously neglected or abused: and they are all hereby earnestly requested to unite the efforts of their voices (however feeble and however uncultivated) to swell the loud and rich note of praise and thanksgiving to God – that so the offering may, to the best of their power, be rendered acceptable to Him, and worthy the creature from whom it emanates."

This contained words only (New Version) and I have ascertained that it was compiled by the local schoolmaster at the time, Mr. W. Bramwell.

W. H. Mason issued a somewhat similar book for Chichester and general use, with a varied version of Tate and Brady's words; this book was used in S. Bersted Church amongst other places.

Another collection made for Chichester's use has a beautifully engraved title-page (herein reproduced) typical of the books of the period. A comparison of this real work of art with the title-page of any modern hymn-book makes one regret the passing of the copper-plate and ashamed of its graceless substitute. Every page of this Chichester psalmody is printed from an engraved plate and the whole work is a joy to the eye as well as to the ear. As will be gathered from the following extracts from the Preface, the compiler was neither financially nor musically ambitious:–

"The Collection has the Approbation of the Minister of our Parish; the Reverend Gentlemen of the Choir have examined the Musical Part; and as the Person who is at the Expense of publishing it has no pecuniary Advantage in View, he therefore hopes it will be kindly received."

"Here are thirteen, plain, good Tunes, and thirty-nine Portions of some of the most useful Parts of the Psalms: If three Psalms be allowed to each Sunday, the Collection will be sung through once in a Quarter."

Another local book has an excellent set of Rules which throw an interesting side-light on the customs of the day:–

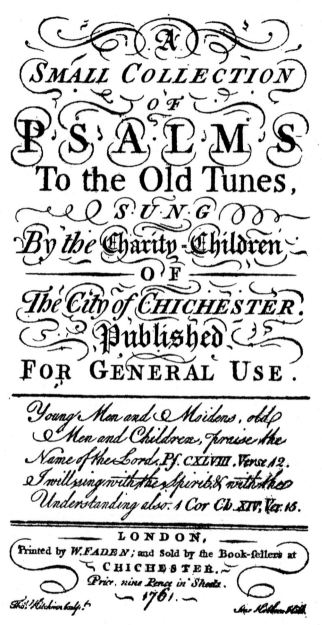

Facsimile of title page of Chichester Psalmody

Psalms and Hymns for the use of Petworth Church Principally selected and adapted by the late Rev. C. Dunster, A.M., Rector of that Parish.

THE RULES

The following Rules are recommended to be observed, in the manner of performing the Psalmody.

1. The Clerk to give out the Psalm, distinctly, in his natural tone of voice,

2. The Organ, or Instrumental Band, to play the tune over once; the last note of which will be the key, or pitch note.

3. The Clerk then to give out the first line of the Psalm, in the key note.

4. Then the Congregation all standing up* to sing the Psalm, within the compass of everyone's voice; and, where there is no Organ, without any instrumental accompaniment, except that of the Violoncello, and of some one other instrument, when it may be found necessary to regulate the voices of the boys.

5. All persons who can sing, are desired to join in the Psalm; singing in unison, unless well skilled in music, so as ably to take another part.

By the observation of these Rules, it is presumed the Psalms may easily be sung by the whole Congregation in such a manner as to render them a most pleasing, affecting and edifying part of the Service.

* This becoming custom is now so general that it is needless to press it: but, it may be here observed, that a large Congregation rising all at once, on the opening of a fine Psalm, and the greater part of them joining devoutly in the Psalmody, has a singularly powerful and influencing effect."

The Bev. C. Dunster was Rector of Petworth from 1789 to 1816.

A special hymn for the Children of Petworth School written by Hayley, the Sussex poet, occurs at the end of Dunster's *Psalms and Hymns for use of Petworth Church*. This is probably unknown to most people and it is worthy of preservation:–

    Saviour! whose tender love and care
    To infant minds exprest,
    Benignly witnessed, that they bear
    Resemblance to the Blest.

    For us the young, who love Thy Name
    And hold Thy promise sure,

O make it our continual aim
To be, as Thou art, pure!

If prone to err, yet quick to mend,
Let this our study be,
Ever to seek a heav'nly Friend
And find that Friend in Thee.

We honour all, who raise our thought
Above the Valley's clod,
All, by whose Bounty we are taught
To know and serve our God.

Mention is made of another Sussex book by the late Rev. E. B. Ellman, Rector of Berwick (Sussex) from 1846 to 1906, in his interesting book of reminiscences, *Recollections of a Sussex Parson*, wherein he states that "The hymnal used at Berwick in 1838 was a local one for the neighbourhood." This may have been a psalmody or hymn-book compiled by Mr. Scobell, of Southover, Lewes, which was introduced into the parish in 1825, but I have been unable to trace any existing copy of this work, or obtain any account of it.

A small collection of *Responses to the Commandments* was published about 1850 by J. Angel, Vicar-choral of Chichester Cathedral, a copy of which is kept in Tangmere Church.

It is now impossible to ascertain the number of churches in which any of these home-born collections were used, but two of them went through several editions and probably most of them were well-known in other parishes besides that of their birth. Unfortunately the old "musicianers" have died out, and their "Ancient and Modern" fed off-spring have too often cared for none of the things of their forbears; few copies of the old psalmodies are now in existence, and even the churches that called them into being know them no more.

Fortunately in another class of tune-book, of far more interest in some respects than the printed ones, specimens are still extant in nearly every parish, many of them in excellent preservation and well-treasured. These are the Manuscript-books written and used by the enthusiastic and painstaking village scribes, who often combined the art of the singer or player with that of the copyist and composer; and if their musical talents were in any way equal to their skill with the pen, they were good musicians indeed. The manuscripts are generally excellent; they are neatly written, the notes are well-formed and mistakes are rare. In some cases the pages are adorned with simple but effective zig-zag lines, dots and scroll-work, betokening a labour of love as well as of necessity.

These MSS. were indeed a necessity to our forefathers, owing to the plain fact that the cost of printed music-books was practically prohibitive to the village choirman, who would have often had to pay as much as a week's wages for a single copy of a tune-book. Each man found it more economical, and far more interesting, to make his own copy; and in most cases this book became a cherished and well-used possession for the rest of the owner's life,

Occasionally, of course, the books, both printed and manuscript, were supplied by the Churchwardens and belonged to them, but more often the individual musicians provided their own music and instruments as well.

Frequently fche old MS. books were 'begun' at both ends, to use an Irishism, the psalm-tunes being written at one end and the anthems at the other, the book having been turned upside-down for the latter purpose. Each tune had its own special name or title, by which it became generally known. No doubt this universal custom of naming tunes, which was first adopted in a printed book by Ravenscroft in his Psalmody issued in 1621, owed its origin to the large number and variety of tune-books that were written or published early in the 17th century, no two of them being quite alike as to pagination or the order in which the tunes occurred. In referring to any particular tune the choirmen found it more convenient to indicate it by name rather than by number or page; and the old musicians always continued to speak of tunes by name, in preference to number, long after the widespread adoption of the two or three best known modern hymn-books had rendered numbers more feasible.

Down to the middle of the 19th century the melodies of all the church-tunes were sung by the Tenor voices, not by the Treble as at the present time. This was a survival of the old custom of giving the plain-song to the Tenor when the ecclesiastical tones were first issued in four parts. An interesting allusion to this custom occurs in a metrical version of the Psalms done by Archbishop Parker and printed for private circulation about 1557. Eight tunes only (the "tones") were issued with this book and prefixed to them is this instruction: " The Tenor of these partes be for the people when they will syng alone, the other partes put for the greater queers [choirs], or to such as will syng or play them privately."

In most of the tune-books of the Past, where the words are printed between the staves of the music, they are placed under the tenor stave alone, thus indicating which was the most important part of the tune.

In 1895 in conversation with an old singer named Pearce at Hurst-pierpoint, who died a few years later when he was over ninety years of age, I asked about the custom of the melody being sung by the tenors, and old Pearce seemed surprised at the question, for he had even then apparently scarcely grasped the fact that the tenors had latterly given way to the trebles in the matter of melody.

A typical manuscript book, of probably late 18th century, was used at Waldron Church by successive generations of the Collins family, members of which still live in the parish. It contains 55 pages of music, all very neatly written, with tunes arranged in 2, 3 or 4 parts. In size it is 11^1/$_4$in. x 9^1/$_2$in., and it is bound in leather, with a piece of old parchment bearing some 16th century writing on it incorporated in the binding. Among the hymns in it is the Christmas Hymn beginning with the line, as it was originally written, "Hark, all around the Welkin ring."

A manuscript book in the possession of Mr. Herbert S. Aylmore, Chichester, was formerly used in St. John's Church, Chichester, and I believe it was written by Thos. Bennett, the compiler of *Sacred Melodies*. Most of the tunes are the same as those contained in the 4th Edition of that work. Several familiar old tunes, well-known by name even in these prosaic days of numbers, have been re-named in this collection: thus, 'Helmsley' is called 'Shopwick'; 'Melcombe' is shorn of the first note in each line and re-named 'Bognor'; Rousseau's 'Dream' is used as a hymn-tune and entitled 'Eartham'; while

Beethoven's Andante from the Sonata in A flat is adapted and dubbed 'Funtington.'

One of the finest MS. books is in the possession of Mr. Herbert Blackman (Hastings) whose father the late Mr. Robert Blackman wrote the music and used it at Catsfield many years ago. All the tunes are perfectly written and the name at the head of each is done in elaborate Old English lettering in splendid style. At the end of the book is a quaint device of two swimming swans in a circle, surrounded by the text "The Lord sitteth above the water flood, Hallelujah." There are four other MS. books belonging to the same owner, one of them with a printed label on it: "Catsfield Choir, 1846."

At Bosham there was a complete set of large MS. books, all dated 1822, for the different voices, bass, etc. A Willingdon book of 18th century contains a fine tune by a local composer. The music in an Angmering book was "very clearly and neatly copied." A Hurst-pierpoint specimen, dated 1829, is a good example of an ornamented music-book. Several well-written manuscripts are preserved in Warnham Church (two dated 1799 and 1812 respectively) in one of which is a tune to 'Trumpet metre' whatever that may mean. A West Grinstead anthem-book has the words placed underneath the tenor part only, which was the part that always had the melody assigned to it in the olden days. The penmanship of a Wilmington MS. of the 18th century, is truly excellent, both notes and words being written with a care that one could scarcely have expected in those illiterate days. The scribe of this book made a mistake in one of the lines of the music and in order to point out his error he has written across the stave in bold letters the word – RONG.

An exceptional example of the illustrative abilities of our old Sussex musicians is given in the title-page of this book. This is the work of Mr. Frederick Jones, of East Hoathly, who played the flute seventy years ago at Falmer and other churches. He was the son of a well-known local singer, and he bad been a church musician, composer, artist and writer for nearly three-quarters of a century; and an enthusiast of the old type, who, alas, are gradually passing away, leaving no-one apparently to take their places. Mr. Jones ornamented many of the old MS. tune-books in bygone years, but as be had none

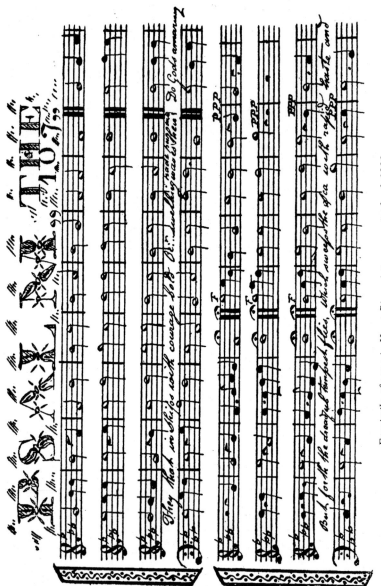

Facsimile of page in Hurst-Pierpoint manuscript book 1829

of them still extant he assayed in this title-block to prove that his right hand had not yet lost its cunning – with what success the reader may judge.

As before stated many of the copyists of tunes were also composers, and not a few of their tunes deserve a better fate than the oblivion in which they now repose. A fine collection was composed by James Marshall, of Rogate, early in the 19th century; they were of a bold and vigorous type and were no doubt very popular. Their names reveal the homeland of the composer – Rogate, Trotton, Elsted, Woolbeding, Harting, Treyford, Iping, etc.

A former organist of West Tarring Church had a MS. book in which he had written the following acrostic on his own name, William Challen:–

"An Acrostick Soliloquy on a Sunday morning,

Wake up my soul, awake arise and sing,
I will arise and. praise my God, my King*
Let us keep this holy day prepare,
Let's to the house of God with joy repair,
In bumble penitence, in thanks and prayer,
And in sweetsacred songs and hymns divine,
May every breathing creature joyful joyn,
Call forth sweet notes, let harmony abound;
Hark how the angels sing and heaven resound,
And thou my soni, quick echo back the sound.
Lo 1 I will gladly touch the trembling chord,
Lo ! I will gladly sing thy praise, 0 Lord,
Ev'n while I live my month shall speak thy praise,
Nor leave me Lord, but guide me in thy ways.
WM. C. 1777,
Organist Tarring Church, 1762."

Mr. Thomas Ralph Hyde, of Worthing, possesses an old MS. book written and used by big great-grandfather, Edward Hyde, who was Churchwarden of Broadwater in 1758. In this book is an excellent address to lovers of music of which the first paragraph runs thus:–

"To all lovers of Divine Musick.

Music, that Divine, Eternal, misterioua art, more boundless than the ocean, inspir'd by God into the hearts of the children of men to land and magnify the great and awfull name of their Creator, is not connn'd to the low limmits of this terrestrial globe (subject to decay) but has its chief residence amongst the glorious company of Saints, Angels, Cherubins and Seraphins, who are continually employing it before the Almighty presence of God and our Lord and Saviour Jesus Christ. Before whose throne (wak'd by the sound of the last trumpet) we shortly must appear, where I hope all true lovers of Divine music will, united, joyn in that heavenly band for ever."

Turning from manuscript to print again we come to the large number of published psalmodies by "foreign" compilers formerly used in Sussex churches. The earliest I have discovered is a small copy of *Day's Psalter* (see illustration p.59). This contains the Old Version, with tunes; it is dated 1630 and entitled – *The Whole Booke of Psalmes Collected into English Meeter by T, Sternhold, I. Hopkins, W. Whittingham conferred with the Hebrew with apt notes to sing them withall. Newly set forth and allowed to be sung in all Churches of all the people together before and after Morning and Evening Prayer, and also before and after Sermons. Moreover in private houses for their godly solace and comfort, laying apart all ungodly songs and ballads which may fend only to the nourishing of vice and the corrupting of youth.*

This book is now in fche possession of Mr. E. Collins, Bramber, and is bound in velvet, with silver filigree ornamentation on the cover; and bound in with it is a New Testament dated 1628. It was formerly used at Waldron (the early home of Mr. Collins) and it contains the Psalms, Canticles, Lord's Prayer, Ten Commandments, etc., done into 'meeter and set to apt notes withall,' the said notes being of the usual diamond shape of the period (See illustration p.81).

The next Sussex book in date is in the Warnham collection: John Playford's *Introduction to Music*, with which is incorporated *The Art of Descant* by Dr. Thos. Campion, dated 1664. This book was at one time the property of Michael Turner, Parish Clerk of Warnham from 1835 to the year of his death in 1885. Previously it belonged to a

Facsimile (³/₄ size) of Old 100th from "The Art of Descant" by T. Campion, 1664

singer of a neighbouring parish whose name is inscribed on the first page in early 18th century style – "May Jephthaniah Mugeridge, Rudgwick." *The Old 100th* appears in *The Art of Descant*; the treble and bass parts alone are given with the usual mark or "direct" at the end of each stave to indicate the note on which the particular part begins in the next line.

Old Michael Turner (portrait p.82) "was a great character in the village of Warnham. He was Master man and leader of the choirband who played in the rood loft, which was removed during the restoration of the Church, unfortunately in 1847, and he always wore a white smock frock, red handkerchief, tie and breeches, and an old-fashioned beaver high hat on Sundays. The viol (or fiddle) was played by

Michael Turner, of Warnham. Born 1796, Died 1885

Michael and we still possess it in the glass case in the vestry. We also had the clarionet until a few years ago when it was unfortunately stolen by a thief who entered the Church at night and took it away with the money from the poor-box which he broke open. We never had a pitch-pipe as far as I can ascertain, but the old steel tuning-fork which Michael used is still preserved with his fiddle.

You will find among the books two of dance-music which Michael used at our village fairs when he used to stand on a tub and played the music for the dances on the green. The description of the rules for the various dances are very amusing. You may be interested with the following lines which I composed and are inscribed on Michael's gravestone – he was actually playing his fiddle when he died–

> His duty done, beneath this stone
> Old Michael lies at rest,
> His rustic rig, his song, his jig
> Were ever of the best.
>
> With nodding head the choir he led,
> That none should start too soon;
> The second too, he sang full true,
> His viol played the tune.
>
> And when at last his age had passed,
> One hundred, less eleven,
> With faithful cling to fiddle string,
> He sang himself to Heaven."   *

Another of the Warnham collection is Evisan's *A Compleat Book of Psalmody*, 1750, similar copies of which were used in Bosham and Lindfield Churches. The former owners of this Bosham book adorned it with their autographs in an interesting manner; thus:–

---

* From letter written to me in 1917 by Mr. C. J. Lucas, of Warnham Court.

"James Wossil His book march y' 27 in the yeare of 1757.
James Wossil His Book,
God give him grace therein to look,
But not to look but understand
That larning is better than house and land;
When land is gone and munny spent,
Then larning is most excellent."

"John Caplin his Book 1791 Harting, Sussex.
John Caplin
His Hand and Pen,
He will be good
But God no [know] when."

"Thomas Welch 1796."
"Elisabeth Welch, Bosham."

The Welch family have lived in the same house in Bosham from father to son for 200 years. They were noted musicians of former days.

Waldron and Warnham churches both used *The Psalmists' New Companion Set forth and corrected by Abraham Adams, at Shoreham in Kent* – an undated book of late 18th century containing Psalm-tunes and Anthems with an Introduction to the *Grounds of Musick*, The preface is a typical example of the ingenuous manner in which the compilers of the old psalmodies lauded their own efforts to improve church music:

"I need not acquaint you with the Original and Ancientness of Music, and of its divine Use, since we have the Testimony of it in Holy Scripture both for Antiquity and Administration in the Church: We cannot doubt of the Inventor thereof since Holy Writ has directed us to Jubal ...

How ravishing and delightful is this Exercise when performed with Skill in a becoming Manner! and how much unlike itself when made up with harsh and disagreeable Sounds. The Design of this Undertaking is to better and improve this excellent and useful Part of our Service, to keep up an Uniformity in our Parish churches, and bring them as much as may be to imitate their Mother-Churches the Cathedrals; so that almost all the Tunes are in tour Parts, being reduced to their proper Keys, and so well adapted to the Words, that all who are capable of Harmony may join in this Consort; and young Men and Maidens, old Men and Children may praise the Name of the Lord.

This will be a Means to add to the Church daily and make us glad to go into the House of the Lord: it will ravish our Hearts with the Harmony of God's Love and Goodness, whilst our Voices are joined in his Praises; that having perfectly learned our Parts here, we may at last come to join with the Heavenly Chorus, and sing Hallelujahs to all Eternity."

A tune-book that was formerly used in Henfield Church has a title-page and introduction typical of the 18th century, thus:–

PSALMODY IMPROVED
Containing upwards of seventy Portions of the
Psalms of David,
and thirteen HYMNS for Particular Occasions, adapted to the best Old and Modern Melodies and some few never before published, with a short Interlude adapted to each.
Also TE DEUM, JUBILATE DEO, CANTATE DOMINO, AND
DEUS MISEREATUR.
(Composed by the Editor)
The whole so adapted as to express in Music, the Accent syllabic Quantity &c. of the Words.
The Words are selected chiefly from the version of Tate & Brady with Amendments by JOHN GRESHAM, Master of the School at Dunstable, and the Music, selected, adapted and composed by
WILLIAM GRESHAM OF DUNSTABLE
PRICE 8s.
Printed for the EDITOR, and sold by PRESTON
97 Strand, London.

This verbose title seems to imply that the Te Deum, Jubilate Deo, etc., were composed by Mr. Gresham and not by King David and others as one is accustomed to believe.

There is a long 'Introduction' to Gresham's book of a boastful nature, though the work itself hardly justifies the boasting. Gresham's interludes may "not seem impertinent" to him, nor perhaps to those who first heard them; but we wonder what the effect would be on a, rustic modern congregation in Sussex if any of them were introduced into a hymn-tune now. Truly, some progress has been made in church music during the last hundred years, in spite of the general adverse criticism of it so prevalent at the present time. 'One of the most dreadful of these interludes, in Psalmody Impioved is introduced into the 'Old 100th'; and both the character of Gresham's 'improvement' to the old tunes and the effect of the interludes themselves may be gathered from the reproduction of that tune herein (see p.87).

The Introduction to Psalmody Improved makes good reading and is here quoted at some length:–

"ON THE WORDS

"The Words are taken from the Version of Tate & Brady with a few alterations; of which the design, in some instances, is to improve the Poetry; in others, to give a Sense nearer to the Prose, or adjust the Words the better to the Music. …

In this selection of Words, the personal pronouns are sometimes made plural by substituting *We* for *I*, *Our* for *My*, a change apparently more adapted to a Congregation of people. For these, and similar reasons, it is hoped the alterations in the Words will not be thought unnecessary or improper.

ON THE MUSIC

As I have before observed, that this Work is intended to promote general singing in Public Worship, then, supposing the plan to be admitted as consistent with propriety, every thing that tends in any degree to obstruct its general reception, should be removed: for this reason I consider *Fugues, Anthems* and *Solos* to be improper; for, though a capital Fugue, as an instrumental piece of Sacred Music, has undoubtedly a very fine effect, yet I cannot think the effect good when performed as a vocal piece of music, in which the Words are repeated many times, and the singers are pronouncing different Words in different parts at the same time – as Dr. Burney says – '*With the clamour of ill-bred disputants, who are talking all at once,*' till the sense of the Sacred Words is entirely sung away, and the performance rendered more like vain babbling, or a confusion of tongues, than an act of Devotion. In many country Churches, I have frequently heard some of the worst portions of the Psalms, from Sternhold & Hopkins' version, sung in ill-constructed Fugues, replete with disallowances or false concords, with the words so broken and half-words repeated and jumbled together in a manner seemingly more calculated to raise the idea of a Catch Club, than to inspire Devotion* … If the words are to be sung and repeated until the sense be lost, it would be equally proper and less profane to sing *Sol la mi fa, &c.*

* I cannot here refrain from giving an instance of this kind of performance … from the 23rd Psalm old version, which was, twelve years ago, a very great favourite with a few ignorant singers at a certain church in

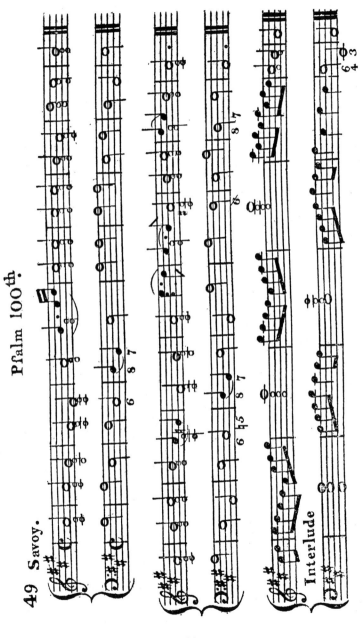

Facsimile of Old 100th in Gresham's 'Psalmody Improved' (date about 1780)

91

Bedfordshire, and which has lately been revived, during the intermission of the Organ, in lieu of Mr. Addison's fine translation of that Psalm. The words are repeated, and the pauses made, in the following manner: *Thou will fill full my cup, and thou – anointed hast my head, anointed hast my head, anointed, nointed hast my head,*

The Tunes which I have selected and composed for this work, will, I hope, be found expressive of the Words to which they are adapted. I likewise think that singing in two parts, Treble or Tenor, and Bass, is preferable to tour parts attempted and not well performed. The usual manner of executing the four parts in country Churches is very singular; for the Air, or principal Part, is uniformly sung by Tenor Voices, and the other two Parts, which should be Accompaniments to the Air and Bass, are sung by Treble and Counter-Tenor Voices; and are thereby frequently rendered too predominant; and, for want of sufficient Voices, the Treble is often omitted, and the Counter made completely to overpower the Air, by being played on a Clarinet or two, and in the Treble Octave.

OF THE PERFORMANCE OF SACRED MUSIC

… The Interludes here introduced are very short, that they may not seem impertinent; but give a respite to the Voices, between the Verses, without interrupting the Sense, which must be the intention of Interludes, and should therefore be omitted where the Sense of the Verse is incomplete."

Instructions as to the rendering of the Psalms are given in *Psalmody Improved* in an amusingly direct manner, thus: *Chearful but not too fast. Loud and not very slow. Supplicating, Loud and Majestic, Slow and Tenderly, Slow and Solemn.*

The frequent repetition of words and phrases of the Psalms, necessitated by the over-wrought tunes of the composers, often led to most 'gigglesome' (an old Sussex word!) absurdities. In Adam's Psalmist's New Companion, which was at one time used at Waldron, the first verse of Psalm CXXVII is thus printed: "Ci. Cities and Holds, Ci. Ci. Cities and Holds, to watch and ward." The syllable Ci. has a minim to itself in one bar, and in another it has a dotted minim with a rest after it. In verse 3 of the same Psalm the words run thus: "Of his great lib., of his great lib., of, of, of his great liberality." Psalm LXXII has: "And the little little little little little little bills."

In Vol, LXII of Sussex Archcæological Collections the Hon. Terence Bourke relates "an amusing story that I had often heard my mother, the late Lady Mayo, tell of Sussex church music of 80 years ago. My mother was a daughter of the first Lord Leconfield, and her memory went back as far as the early thirties of the last century. She used to say she remembered singing in Church every Sunday a version of the Psalms to the accompaniment of a fiddle, a flute and a trombone. A sentence, a word, or a syllable used to be reiterated to fit in with the tune. She and her brothers used to look forward to one particular sentence which was always sung as follows:– My poor pol, My poor pol, My poor polluted heart."

Perhaps the most ludicrous of all these repetitions was one of which the Rev. F. A. Haines, of Sidlesham, has been my informer. An old friend of his many years ago attended a London chapel where the congregation were physically and sentimentally edified in this manner;–

> Oh take thy mourning pil.,
> Oh take thy mourning pil.,
> Oh take thy mourning pilgrim home!

The introduction to Rippon's Tune-book states:–

> ... "Repeated inquiries have been made for tunes suited to many of the Hymns, especially such as are in peculiar metres. These inquiries have been partly answered, some- times by mentioning one Author, and then another; but the purchase and use of several Tune Books being found inconvenient, it was thought that One Volume might be published which should remedy this evil, contain a greater variety than any other book extant – and be calculated to unite London and the Country in singing."

This laudable effort to provide unity between the Capital of England and the Provinces can scarcely have had the desired effect, if we may judge from the contemporary and later prefaces of other tune-books, which continued to bemoan the low state of church music long after Rippon's time.

A familiar survival of the repetitions of words and phrases, though not of the same witless nature, occurs in most modern hymn-books in such hymns as: "O come, all ye faithful," "Lo! He comes," and "All

Dorcheſter Tune.   P S A L M XV.   *Old Verſion.*

2 The man whoſe life is uncorrupt, whoſe works are juſt and ſtrait ;
   Whoſe heart doth think the very truth, and tongue ſpeaks no deceit.
3 That to his neighbour doth no ill, in body, goods, or name ;
   Nor willingly doth ſlanders raiſe, which might impair the ſame.

Facsimile of p.48 of Evisan's 'A Compleat Book of Psalmody', date 1750

Continued.

4 That in his heart regardeth not malicious wicked men:
But thofe that love and fear the Lord, he maketh much of them.
5 His oath, and all his promifes, that keepeth faithfully,
Altho' he make his cov'nant fo that he doth lofe thereby.

G   *Meefbam*

Facsimile of p.49 of Evisan's 'A Compleat Book of Psalmody', date 1750

hail the power," wherein repeats are made at the end of each verse.

Very often the lengthy phrases of music in some of the too elaborate tunes had short words or syllables alloted to them, and the printers often adopted quaint methods of dividing the letters or syllables to fit the music. A specimen tune from Evisan's *Compleat Book of Psalmody*, published in 1750, is reproduced on the two previous pages, and it will be seen that the word 'thy' is thus printed 'th - - - y.' Other instances in the same book are 'heal - - - th,' 'shou - - - ld,' 'b - - - e,' 'th - - - em,' 'ma - - - g - - - ni - - - fy,' 'yo - - - u' 't - - - o.'

The tune from Evisan's book is a fair example of many of the Psalm-tunes of the Past, both in its style and in the way in which the lines of the verses were divided between the four parts of the choir, with the last line or two repeated together. Not all the tunes were thus spread out, but when they were the opening line was almost invariably given out by the tenor or bass.

Allusion has already been made to the common custom of limiting the number of verses of a psalm or hymn to four only. It was apparently a matter a indifference whether the fourth verse made a satisfactory termination or not. Many of the old psalmodies recognised the custom by printing four verses of each psalm, and no more.

The Old or New Version of the Psalms was generally bound in with the copies of the Book of Common Prayer issued in the 17th, 18th and early part of 19th centuries. One such Prayer Book, dated 1716, formerly used in Selsey is full of quaint illustrations, depicting scenes of the Gospels, &c. One picture, in the Form of Thanksgiving for James Ist's deliverance from Gunpowder Plot, shows Guy Fawkes with his lantern going to the Houses of Parliament, while the Eye of God looks down on him from the clouds. Another woodcut (here reproduced) shows David composing the Psalms to very modern-looking music.

Other choir-books formerly used in Sussex churches were:–William's *New Universal Psalmodist,* 1770, at Billingshurst, *Psalms and Hymn-tunes* by Reinagle, at Hellingly; Cheetham's *Psalmody,* 1851, at, Twineham; *The Union Tune Book* at Berwick;

Hornes' *Psalms and Hymns* at Angmering and Hellingly; Rippon's *Tunes* at Wilmington, Lurgashall, Poling and other places; *Congregational Harmonist* and Clark's *Psalms* at Bolney; Mercer's *Church Psalter and Hymn-book*, 1859, at Chiddingly and Hurst-pierpoint; Dr. Addington's *Collection of Psalm-tunes*, 1786, at Waldron; *Bristol Tune-book*, 1863, and Bennett and Goldschmidt's *Chorale Book*, 1863, at several places; *Double Cottage Hymn-book* at Chiddingly, Laughton, Upper Dicker; S.P.C.K. *Selection of Old and New Version*, 1839, at Beddingbam, Bishopstone, Berwick, Seaford, etc.; Hall's *Collection* at Firle; Monk's *Tune-book* at Firle, Rype,

Seaford, etc.; Tolhurst's *Anthems* at Falmer; Bird's *100 Chants* at Dicker; B. Jacob's *National Psalmody*, 1820, at Arundel; *The Seraphine or Sacred Harmonist* at Ashurst; *National Psalmody*, 1844, by H. Forbes, at Henfield; Addison's *Hymns* at Findon; *Beauties of Sacred Melody* by J. Alexander (about 1820) at Selsey; *Anthems and Psalm-tunes* by W. H. Burgess, 1832, at Stedham; *Anthems and Psalms*, by Tolhurst, at Stedham and other places (Anthem No. 1 in this book is headed "Proper on Sacrament Days"); *Psalms and Hymns* published by J. Mallett in 1839, at Selmeston; Joule's *Chants*, 1860, and Turle's *Chant-book*, 1865, at Tangmere. The dates given in this list refer either to the year of publication of the book, or to the time when they were in use in the respective parishes. The metrical versions of the Psalms in most of these collections were either Sternhold & Hopkins, or Tate & Brady, and the hymns were largely from Dr. Watts. A copy of the words only of S. and H, Version, dated 1744, is at Greatham Church.

On March 20th, 1861, appeared the first edition with tunes of *Hymns Ancient and Modern*; and with the advent of that notable work, practically all the old psalmodies and hymn-books were swept out of the churches of Sussex for ever.

Table of Musical Instruments used in Sussex Churches in the Past.

An asterisk * signifies that the instruments thus indicated are still in existence.

Churches	Flutes	Clarionets	Oboes	Bassoons	Cornets	Trombones	Serpents	Violins	'Cellos or Bass-viols	Barrel-organs	Pitch-pipes	Various
Alciston											1*	
Albourne										1		Flutina
Aldingbourne	1	1		1	1			1	1			
Alfriston				5								Several
Amberley		1										Several
Angmering	1								1*	1		
Apuldram								1				
Ashurst	1	1										Double-bass Vamphorn*
Balcombe	1	1						1	1			
Beeding, Upper							1*					
Bersted										1		
Berwick	2							1	1		1	Cornopean
Bignor		1						2				
Billingshurst	2							1	1			Pitchfork
Birdham		1				1		2				Several
Bishopstone										1		Several
Bolney	1*								1*	1		
Bosham	1	1*		1				2	1*		1*	
Boxgrove	1	1						3	1	1		
Brede											1*	
Brightling	1			1				1	1	1*		Banjo
Broadwater		1*		1*							1*	
Buxted	1	1						1	1			
Catsfield	1*											
Chiddingly	1											
Chichester Cathedral											1*	
Clymping	2							2	1			
Cocking	1	1							1			Seraphim
Cuckfield	1	1*							1			
Ditchling											1*	
Donnington	2	1							1	2		Double-bass
Eastbourne												Double-bass
Eastergate	1									1		
Falmer	2		1	1				2	1	1	1	Double-bass
Felpham		1							1			
Fernhurst										1		
Ferring	1	1*,1		1*				1	1	1	1	
Findon	1	1						1	1		1	
Firle										1		
Fishbourne, New	1	1			1			3				
Funtington										1		Fife
Glynde	1											
Goring		1			1						1	
Grinstead, West	1	1		1				2	2	1	1	
Guestling										1		
Hailsham		1		1								French-horn
Hartfield										1		
Harting		1*						1	1	1		
Heathfield	1	1		2		1						Bass-horn
Hellingly	1			1	1			4	1			

Churches	Flutes	Clarionets	Oboes	Bassoons	Cornets	Trombones	Serpents	Violins	'Cellos or Bass-viols	Barrel-organs	Pitch-pipes	Various
Henfield	1	1*			2	1		1	1	1	1	
Hoathly, East	1	1						1	1		1	
Hooe									1*			
Ifield										1		
Jevington										1		
Lavant, East	2*										1*	
Lindfield	1*	2*		1*				1*	1			
Lodsworth	1	1				1		1			1	Kettledrum
Lurgashall								4				
Mayfield				1			1					
Newick	1											
North Chapel		1								1	1*	
Northiam	1											
Nuthurst	1	1						1	1*			Drum
Oving										1		
Pagham										1		
Parham										1*		
Piddinghoe										1*		
Poling	1*	1*				1		2	1			
Pulborough										1		
Roffey	1	1						1	1			Drum
Rogate	2*	1						2	1	1	1	
Rotherfield										1		
Rustington		1						1	1			Triangle
Rye								1	1			
Salehurst										1	1	
Selham	1							1				
Selmeston											1*	
Selsey	1*			1			1	2*	1		1	Fife*
Sennicotts										1		
Shermanbury	1*,1								1*			
Shipley										1		
Sidlesham		1*	1*	1*				1*			1*	
Singleton	1					1		1		1		
Stanmer										1		
Stedham	1	1		1*		1		1			1	
Steyning										1		
Stopham										1		
Sutton								2				
Tangmere										1		
Tarring, West	1	2*,3	1*	2*		1		1	2		1*	
Thakeham										1		
Twineham	1							2	1		1	
Wadhurst	1	1						1	1*	1		
Waldron	2	2		1					2			
Wannock										1		
Warbleton										1		
Warnham		1						1*	1			
Westbourne		1							2			
Weshampnett					1							
Willingdon	1	1		1				1		1	1	
Wilmington	1	1							1		1	
Withyham	1	1		2				3	2			
Wittering, East	3	3						1	1			
Wittering, West		1										
Woodmancote	1	1			1	1		1				
Yapton				1								

CHURCHES WHERE BANDS WERE USED
BUT INSTRUMENTS UNKNOWN:–

Coombes, Fernhurst, Ifield, Lancing, Patcham, Preston, Shipley, Sompting, Thakeham, Tillington.

Birdham, Bishopstone and Newick had several other instruments. Brightling is said to have had 9 bassoons.

At Heathfield the blacksmith played a bassoon which he called a "sacbut."

At Lindfield a harp was used for choir practices but not at the services.

Alciston and Selmeston used the same pitchpipe.

A pitchpipe in the possession of Mr. Garraway Rice, F.S.A., was purchased by him from a man in Pulborough, where it had probably been used.

INDEX

THE MACDERMOTT COLLECTION OF

SUSSEX MUSIC

In 1925 Canon K. H. Macdermott, the author of Sussex Church Music in the Past (Chichester, 1922), presented to the Sussex Archaeological Society three instruments formerly used in Sidlesham Church: a Longman and Broderip oboe of 1791, a clarionet by Cramer and a bassoon by Metzler. He has now presented to the Society all the materials which he has gathered in the course of a lifetime's researches into the history of Church music and instruments in Sussex. These include two bulky MS. books in which information from over 120 villages is compiled in alphabetical order; a remarkable collection of old Psalters and Hymn Books published for the use of individual parishes; and a number of fascinating MS. books of secular music – country dances, marches, songs – compiled mainly at the close of the eighteenth and the beginning of the nineteenth century.

Apart from the MacDermott bequest the Society also possesses a bassoon formerly used in Ditchling Church; more recently (1952) it has been presented with a piccolo, with alternative flageolet mouthpiece, used in Catsfield Church in the 1840s by the great-grandfather of the donor, Mr. Poulter of Chilworth; finally, a handsome home-made fiddle by James Nye of Lewes (1863). The Society therefore already has the nucleus of what it is hoped will gradually develop into a representative survey of the county's musical history. Canon MacDermott's work is unique, for music-making in no other county has so far been investigated with such thoroughness. Those who possess his book may like to know, however, that since it was published a number of instruments have been restored to Sussex churches in addition to those listed on pp. 91 and 92 in Sussex Church Music in the Past,

He has himself restored a small fife to Sidlesham Church (May, 1953); Wilmington Church now possesses the flute used 160 years

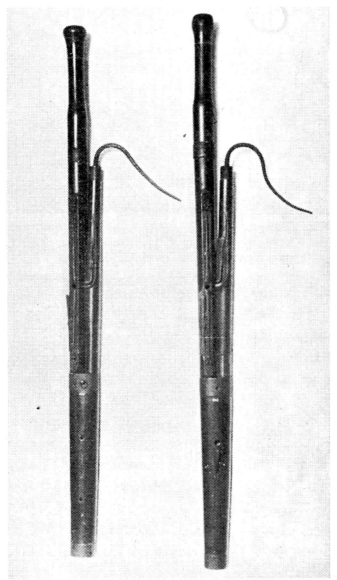

*Left to right: A bassoon used in Sidlesham Church, presented to the Sussex
Archaeological Society by Canon MacDermott, and a bassoon used in Ditchling
Church, lent to the Sussex Archaeological Society by Mr. James Nye*

ago by the Clerk, Mr. Crowhurst (presented by his nephew's widow in 1939); Henfield Church has had, since 1941, an oboe, violin, clarionet and flute formerly used in its church orchestra; Brede has a clarionet played by J. Ellis in the 1820s. A number of these old instruments remain in private hands, including the bassoon and flute once played in Hailsham Church. It is to be hoped that in time they will all be restored to the churches where they were played with such devotion and enthusiasm before the inception of the organs and harmoniums, or, better, perhaps, added to the Archaeological Society's collection in Barbican House.

Certain parts of the county appear to have been particularly thriving centres of village church music. Even after the break up of the old church bands, the members sometimes continued to meet for their own private enjoyment. Thus, correspondence which Canon MacDermott had with the son of an old flautist in Catsfield Church shows that he had himself "seen some of the old veterans meet at my father's house and heard them sing – the Collect for the 7th Sunday after Trinity, as an anthem, was their favourite." The enthusiasm of the Catsfield "musickers" is further attested by the eight MS. books of psalm tunes and anthems which survive from this church (most of them in Barbican House). It is moving to delve into these lovingly inscribed compilations of music, though, it must be admitted, this has little intrinsic merit, for by our modern standards of church music taste was low in the heyday of the church bands.

More important than the quality of the music (and the village musicians could hardly be blamed for the universally low level of taste which prevailed in the first half of the nineteenth century) is the fact that in every village the bands were making their own music in church week by week. Certainly, their disbandment did not necessarily raise the standard of taste. As Hardy said, it meant the disappearance of "an important union of interests," and it is arguable that the Church had a much stronger influence in the villages when these faithful bands, rather than a solitary organist or harmonium-player, were responsible for the music.

This was one of the points made by Lucy Broadwood, the great Sussex folksong scholar, in the correspondence with Canon

110

MacDermott which forms not the least valuable item in the collection of materials he has presented to Barbican House. She wrote to him in 1925:
"Nowadays, when musical festivals have leavened the villages and small towns in most parts of England, it might be possible to get together a musicianly little church orchestra, since villagers can usually have music teaching if they choose."

Such teaching is of course now easily available through the Rural Music School but so far as I know no regular orchestra has been instituted in any Sussex church. The nearest approach to a restitution of the old church orchestras appears to have been provided by the group of Sussex Recorder Players who accompanied the services held in the summer months in 1952 and 1953 in Hamsey Church, now without a musical instrument of any kind. Lucy Broadwood's letters

A page from the tune book compiled by the Welch family of Bosham.
Note alternative title: "Harriet Martin's Fancy," showing the use of
"Auld Lang Syne" as a dance

include an amusing picture of church "music" in Rusper Church in the early 1870s, where, before her own appointment as organist at the age of fourteen, the services were unaccompanied.

"The only music" (she wrote) "was unaccompanied. Mr. Gore (the parson) gave several astonishingly loud coughs and, having announced the number of the hymn, started it in any key that came uppermost in his mind in a very piercing nasal tone like that of a bagpipe. When Mr. Gore pitched too high or too low the effects were very funny. But, I am grateful for this queer experience, for 'O come, O come, Emanuel,' sung in rough unison took such a hold on me that I date my love for 'modes' and plainsong from hearing the villagers shout that tune... Alas, the day came when an American organ was presented to Rusper Church and I, as a girl of 14, was made organist. There were some 5 or 6 boys and a man or two in white smocks who sang (in very harsh unmelodious tones) in the so-called 'choir'; and strangers used to think we had a 'surpliced choir.'

Our old clerk, Fairbrother, was a lovely old man, with the blue eyes, fresh complexion and aquiline features of the fine Sussex stock. I can hear him now, sitting in the 'churching-pew,' responding in clear accents on behalf of the timid woman at his side. In Rusper Vestry was a fine old Parish Chest cut out of a solid oak trunk. This became unduly full of registers; so one day Fairbrother burnt a large number of the oldest. Mr. Gore was not good at accounts. He mixed Debit and Credit and added them up together. If a Clothing or Coal Club account puzzled others in consequence, he – though a very poor man – was eager to pay out of his own pocket in order to square things."

In another letter she vividly describes a traditional Sussex Morris dancer whose performance she witnessed in the 1870s, unaware at the time that he was anything more than a "modernised country lad imitating the Christy Minstrels."

"I was lunching alone at Lyne (Rusper), my old home, when – it was May Day – there appeared on the carriage drive a man with a blackened face. He had a white shirt and ribbons and fringes of paper on him. He danced in a circle, leaping high in the curious

Left to right, (a) The leather case used to hold the Catsfield piccolo (c), (b) a violin made by James Nye of Lewes in 1863, (c) a piccolo with alternative flageolet mouthpiece used in Catsfield church in the 1840's.
Presented to the Sussex Archaeological Society by Mr. T. Poulter

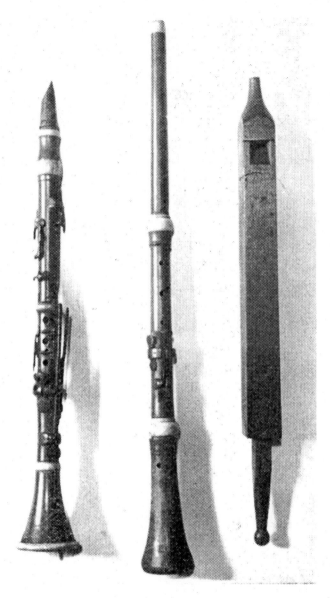

Left to right: A clarinet used in Sidlesham Church, an oboe used in Sidlesham Church and a pitch pipe once used in an unspecified Sussex church. All presented to the Sussex Archaeological Society by Canon MacDermott

'caper' which seems traditional in many countries, one leg tossed in the air with a sharply bent knee. As he bounded in this circular fashion he blew on a cow's horn, which made a most uncanny barbarous sound. ... Later I realised I had seen my one and only Sussex morris-caperer. Was he perhaps a gypsy?"

It is so rare to hear of Morris dancing in Sussex in the nineteenth century that this account is of historical interest. Incidentally, a cow's horn was also used in the old Sussex custom of "wassailing" apple trees at Christmas.

For the historian of church music the MacDermott collection of early Sussex psalters and hymn books is of great interest and importance. It is surprising how many parishes had their own specially printed collections. The earliest example in the collection is *A small collection of Psalms to the old Tunes sung by the Charity Children of the City of Chichester* (Chichester, 1761), containing "13 plain good tunes." Next in date is a collection of *Psalms, Hymns and Anthems sung in the Parish Church of Burwash* (Tunbridge Wells, 1790). The first Lewes example represented is the Hymns compiled by Joseph Middleton, 1793 ("Sold by the compiler at Lewes"). The early nineteenth century collections include *Hymns occasionally sung at the Church of St. Pancras, Rumboldswyke* (Chichester 1810) compiled by the Rector of Rumboldswyke, William Walker (1774-1827), who, in the Preface, protests against the custom of "joining in the delightful exercise of psalmody in a lolling position better suited to the levities of the theatre." W. Figg of Lewes published *Psalms selected from the New Version for the use of St. Michaels and other Parishes in and about Lewes and Brighton* in 1811, and in 1815 there appeared *Psalms and Hymns selected for the use of the Chapel of Ease, Worthing.* (It was an organist of this Chapel who collaborated with the Rev. John Broadwood, Lucy Broadwood's uncle, in the epoch-making collection of Sussex Songs published in 1843). Selections of Psalms and Hymns for use in the Parish churches of Warbleton and Northiam appeared in 1828.

William Figg of Lewes, compiler of the collection mentioned above, was a noted land surveyor, and his son, also a surveyor, was one of the founders of the Sussex Archaeological Society and the author of many papers in the Society's *Collections* notably "Some Memorials of Old Lewes" in Vol. XIII. Messrs. Ernest H. Fuller of 19 High Street, Lewes now hold the important collection of Maps and Plans accumulated by William Figg (and begun by his father). Grandfather, father and son were all holders of the office of high-constable in their successive generations. The Figg family appears to have been connected primarily with the Church of St. John sub Castro (cf. "List of Pews from a plan made in 1807 and copied by William Figg in 1816" in *Sussex Notes and Queries*, August 1942, page 55 ff.).

These printed collections were probably beyond the resources of most of the church "musickers" and they made their own MS collections. Apart from the Catsfield collections already mentioned (all dated 1846) those to be seen in Barbican House include a compilation by John Wells of Lindfield, an especially handsome collection by John Bailey of Ringmer (1832) and others from Uckfield (1813) and Wilmington (no date).

The earliest and most interesting of the MS. collections dates from 1796 and was made by William Aylmore of West Wittering. Unlike the other MS. tune-books this one is entirely devoted to country dances and marches. Many of the tunes are arranged for two clarinets and the compiler was in all probability a clarinettist in West Wittering Church. The book was given to Canon MacDermott by Mary Goodger of Funtington in 1917 and she stated that "my grandfather used to play the clarinet in West Wittering Church" (he was therefore presumably Aylmore's partner in these arrangements for two clarinets).

Of William Aylmore himself considerable research has only revealed that a William Aylmore, who was probably the clarinettists son, died at the age of eighty-one in 1851 – a farmer who was "respected by all his neighbours rich and poor" (*Sussex Advertiser*, 11th November, 1851). I am, however, indebted to Mr. Challen of Worthing for the information that a William Aylmore (also a farmer) died in either 1804 or 1803.

The MS. book contains two dates: 1796 and 1818, both apparently in the same hand, but if the compiler in fact died in 1803 or 1804 the second date may have been inscribed by his son who died in 1851. Most of the country dances appear in other collections of the time but the only other source to which I have traced *What a Beau my Granny Was* is Add. MS. 25073 in the British Museum. (*Country Dances of the Year* 1790). Some of the marches occur rarely in other sources, a few, apparently, not at all. Thus the *Light Horse March* only occurs elsewhere in a MS. in the Kidson Collection, as I am informed by Dr. Henry Farmer, the leading authority on military band music. *George Roley's March* has so far eluded detection in any other source.

Two MS. books compiled by the Welch family of Bosham, who lived in the same house in direct succession for 270 years, combine secular with sacred tunes. The larger of the two compilations, which is dated 1822, follows up William Croft's hymn-tune *Hanover* (here attributed to "Handel") with *Rule Britannia* and *Rockingham* ("When I survey the wondrous Cross") with the rollicking *Water Loo Fair*. Country dances such as *Speed the Plough* jostle with popular songs such as *Lillyferlero* (sic) and *The Bluebells of Scotland*. Hornpipes abound in the collection but waltzes and quicksteps were obviously becoming popular too. The compiler was probably the village fiddler who played for dancing and singing as well as in the church orchestra.

As Canon MacDermott noted in *Bosham Church: its History and Antiquities* (Chichester, 1911), Bosham has been "decidedly of a musical bent" for generations. This MS. collection of the Welch family certainly reflects the versatile tastes of one of its oldest families. The MacDermott bequest also includes another heirloom of the Welch family: Thomas Welch's copy of *The Kentish Divine Harmonist* by John Barwick of Canterbury, in which the owner inscribed the following curious verse (dated 1811):

"When drest for the evening the girls nowadays
Scarce an atom of dress on them leave;
Nor blame them for what is an evening dress,
If it be not suited to eve."

Finally, the collection contains a volume of Thompson's *Complete Collection of 200 favourite Country Dances* which bears the inscription: "Walter Burt a prentic to a farrier, June the 23, 1781." A later owner (1787) inscribed the following:

"Elizabeth Goldsmith is my name and englon is my Nasshon

Albourn is my dwelling plaas and Christ is my salvashan
And when the bell for me douth towl Lord Jesus
Christ recev my soul.
Elizabeth Goldsmith rote this Nov. 15 in 1787."

The copy is imperfect; it begins at page 11 of the Index. A letter from Cecil Sharp enclosed in the volume suggests that it is Volume IV of Thompson's series of country dance publications and the present writer has confirmed this by comparison with other extant copies.

The only other Sussex collection at all comparable to the MacDermott Collection which now has its home in Lewes, is that of Michael Turner of Warnham, which includes Playford's rare *Introduction to Music* of 1664 with his *Introduction to the Playing of the Viol* and Campion's *The Art of Descant*, and also two of Turner's own MS. books of dance tunes. Turner was a well-known fiddler (Parish Clerk of Warnham from 1835-1885). It would be a convenience for students to have his collection incorporated with the MacDermott collection but these things were part and parcel of his life and it is appropriate that they should remain in Warnham with his fiddle. On the other hand, it is to be hoped that the existence of this substantial collection of documents of the county's musical past will stimulate others to search for and present new additions.

From an article by Stanley Godwin
Vol. XXVIII Sussex County Magazine pp58-163

HOPE IN THE VALLEY CD

These carols were collected and collated by Dr Vic Gammon. This performance by 'Hope in the Valley' – a group of singers and musicians from all over Sussex, and directed by Mary Motley. It was recorded in the Spring of 1983 by Mike Howell. The recording is dedicated to the memory of John Ticehurst, a founder member of the group who died in January 1983.

THE DITCHLING CAROL
Music by Peter Parsons, shoemaker of Ditchling, who died in 1901 aged 76.

HORSHAM TIPTEERS' CAROL
Arranged by Vic Gammon. Sung by mummers in the neighbourhood of Horsham 1878-81.

THEN LET US BE MERRY
From a manuscript written by William Harris, the blacksmith of Rodmell, 1842.

THE SINNER'S REDEMPTION
Arranged by Vic Gammon. From the singing of William Lanning, Terwick, 1911.

BLOW YE THE TRUMPETS
From John Bailey of Ringmer's manuscript book, started 1833.

HARK, HARK WHAT NEWS
Sam Willet, 'the singing baker of Cuckfield' communicated this to Lucy Broadwood in 1901.

THE FALMER CAROL
Communicated by Fred Jones to MacDermott.

On Christmas Night All Christians Sing

Arranged by Vic Gammon. Tune from Mrs Cranston of Billingshurst, 1907. Text from George Night of Horsham and Mrs Verral of Monksgate.

The Comton Tipteers's Carol

Arranged by Vic Gammon. From *The Wonderful Weald* by Arthur Beckett.

The Burwash Carol For Christmas Day

Claimed for John Fleming by his grand-children, and still sung by old men in 1932.

Wake Ye Shepherds

From the manuscript of William Voice of Handcross.

Come All Ye Worthy Christian Men

Arranged by Vic Gammon. From the singing of Henry Hills of Lodsworth.

Shepherds Arise

From the singing of the Copper family of Rottingdean.

COUNTRY BOOKS/ASHRIDGE PRESS

Country Books/Ashridge Press is a small independent publisher producing reprints of scarce and out-of-print classics on Sussex.

BLACK'S 1861 GUIDE TO SUSSEX Incorporating 1859 Breads's guide to Worthing and a description of the Miller's Tomb on Highdown Hill
Folding map of the county and steel engravings of the chain pier at Brighton, Hastings and Chichester Cathedral. Major towns are covered as well as the smaller villages.
Paperback 210 x 148mm 276 pages Engravings and folding map
2000 Country Books ISBN 1 898941 21 1 Price **£8.95**

SHEPHERDS OF SUSSEX by Barclay Wills
Written as the last shepherds were disappearing from the rural scene, with notes on Michael Bland, John Dudeney, etc. Foreword by the Duke of Norfolk. The hill shepherd; lure of the shepherd's work; a character study of Sussex shepherds; shepherds of bygone days; the shepherd's possessions; crooks & bells; shearing; sheep washing, marking & watering; dew-ponds; Sussex sheep; the crow-scarer, etc. A facsimile of the first edition published c1933.
185 x 125mm 280 pages 28 B&W photos
2001 Country Books Hardback ISBN 1 898941 60 2 Price **£20.00**
Paperback ISBN 1 898941 67 X Price **£8.95**

SMUGGLING AND SMUGGLERS IN SUSSEX by 'A gentleman of Chichester'
The inhuman and unparalleled murders of Mr William Galley, a customs house officer, and Mr Daniel Chater, a shoemaker, fourteen notorious smugglers, with the trials and execution of seven of the criminals at Chichester 1748-9. Trials of John Mills and Henry Sheerman; and the trials at large of Thomas Kingsmill for breaking open the Custom House at Poole; also an article on 'Smuggling in Sussex' by William Durrant Cooper, Esq.
Hardback 185 x 125mm 280 pages Engravings
2001 Country Books ISBN 1 898941 61 0 Price **£20.00**

THE HISTORY AND ANTIQUITIES OF HORSHAM by Howard Dudley
First published in 1836. Illustrated with lithographs and wood engravings, the book covers the market town of Horsham and the surrounding villages of Rusper, Warnham, Roffy, Nuthurst, Itchingfield, Slinfold and Rudgwick. The parish church, the county gaol, the Independent's chapel, the Wesleyan chapel, Collier's School, the National School, the Royal British Schools, the great houses and estates, the dragon in St Leonard's Forest, a list of Horsham inns, details of coaches, plants found in the area, fossils, population, roads, Horsham fairs, etc.
Paperback 190 x 125mm 112 pages
2001 Country Books ISBN 1 898941 72 6 Price: **£9.50**

A DICTIONARY OF THE SUSSEX DIALECT by Rev WD PARISH
The dictionary was first published in 1875 by the vicar of Selmeston, the Rev WD Parish. He also recorded provincialisms in use in the county at that time. This new edition is augmented by further pieces on the Sussex dialect, traditional recipes, and a mumming play from West Wittering from the writings of EV Lucas, who died in 1938. Illustrated throughout with line drawings of Sussex views made in the late 19th and early 20th centuries by Frederick L Griggs.

Paperback 220 x 150mm) portrait 192 pages 70 line drawings
2001 Country Books ISBN 1 898941 68 8 Price **£7.50**

HANGED FOR A SHEEP: BYGONE CRIME IN SUSSEX by Dick Richardson
This book surveys crime and the treatment of criminals in bygone Sussex, illustrated with extracts
from late 18th century copies of the Sussex Weekly Advertiser, the county's first weekly newspaper.. "You may as well be hanged for a sheep as a lamb."The saying dates back to the days when
sheeep-stealing was punishable by death. For stealing a lamb you would be "hanged by the neck
until you were dead." The same punishment was meted out for stealing a sheep, so you ran no
greater risk for stealing the more valuable article. (This law was repealed in 1828.)
Paperback size: 210 x 148mm 80 pages. Engravings, woodcuts and photographs.
2003 County Books ISBN 1 898941 85 8 Price **£6.95**

OUR SUSSEX PARISH by Thomas Geering
Arthur Beckett declared that *Our Parish* by Thomas Geering was his favourite Sussex book, first
published in 1884. Thomas Geering was born in Hailsham in 1813 and lived his whole life in the
town. His father, also Thomas Geering, came from Alfriston where he had begun his working life
as a shepherd's boy and a ploughboy before becoming a shoemaker. In November 1812 he
married Elizabeth Holman, the eldest daughter of a yeoman of Hellingly, in the Ebenezer Chapel
at Alfriston and in the following year they moved to Hailsham. Most of the pieces that make up
this book first appeared in the columns of a country newspaper. *The Old Sussex Bookseller,* has
never appeared in book form and was first printed in the *Sussex County Magazine* 1927.
Paperback size: 210 x 148mm 232 pages. 16 photographs.
2003 Country Books ISBN 1 898941 83 1 Price: **£9.95**

THE HISTORY OF DITCHLING IN THE COUNTY OF SUSSEX by Henry Cheale, Jun.
Facsimile of the first edition of 1901. An invaluable document for those searching their family tree.
Alfred the Great and Catherine of Aragon both owned manors in the village. On the basis of this,
the author believed that the king spent much time here and that "Wings Place" or the "Old House"
is a fragment of a palace built by Queen Catherine! Ignoring these flights of fancy, the book is
otherwise thoroughly researched. Contents include: Ancient Ditchling and the manors, Ditchling
Park, old inhabitants, miscellaneous notes, St Margaret's Church, rectors and vicars, monumental
inscriptions and memorials, the Meeting House, the 'Jernal' of a Ditchling man, and the
neighbourhood. Subsidy rolls 1378-9 for Ditchling, Strete Hundred 1549, Ditchling 1562, 1600,
1623, Ditchling wills at Lewes 1541-1640, Ditchling administrators 1578-1640, Ditchling
Churchwardens 1638-1750. The appendices include: family trees of the Chatfield family, the
Attrees of Wivelsfield and the Pooles.
Paperback 183 x 125mm 184 pages. 12 illustrations by Arthur B Packham.
2004 Country Books ISBN 1 898941 89 0 Price: **£9.95**

THE MISTRESS OF STANTONS FARM by Marcus Woodward
First published 1938. Sussanah Hooker was born in 1814 at Smallfield Place, Surrey. She married
Mr Stacey of Stantons and ruled her household at East Chiltington with a rod of iron. She died in
1893 and is buried at Westmeston in East Sussex. There is an introduction by Arthur Beckett.
Contents include: Receipts for Food for the Poor, Life at the Farm, Directions to Servants,
Ornaments for Grand Entertainments, The Doctor, The Squire, The Parson, Grandma, the
Sorceror, Pickles, Preserves and Candies, Grandma's Herb Garden, Vegetables and Herbs, Rural

Worthies, Cullis, Sauces and Eggs, Grandma holds her Court, Distilling Cordial Waters, The Good Things of Sussex, Puddings and Savouries, etc., Wine-Making Day, Home-made wines, Punches, etc., A Tale of a Wash-Tub, Family Receipts, Baking Day, Baked Puddings, etc., The Household Gods, Necessary Knowledge, Christmas Gambols, Creams and Syllabubs, The Sign of the Old Thatch, Buns, Black Caps, and Snow Balls, etc.
Paperback 210 x 148mm 187 pages. Black and white photosgraphs
2004 Country Books ISBN 1 898941 88 2 Price: **£9.95**

RECOLLECTIONS OF A SUSSEX PARSON by Rev. Edward Boys Ellman
First published 1912. Edward Boys Ellman was born in 1815 and was rector of Berwick, East Sussex, for sixty years. A keen observer of life and people, this is a fascinating portrait of life in a small village in the 19th century. Among other humourous incidents is the installation of the barrel organ in the church – that insisted on playing secular tunes, and the lady in Lewes, who asked the shopkeeper to trim a yard off the bottom of a dress while she saved up for it! He died on 22nd February 1906. Index of surnames and place-names.
Paperback 210 x 148mm 269 pages. Photographs and line drawings.
2004 Country Books ISBN 1 898941 87 4 Price: **£9.95**

A SOUTHDOWN FARM IN THE 1860's by Maude Robinson of Saddlescombe
Maude Robinson was born in May 1859 at Saddlescombe where her father, Martin Robinson, had a 900-acre farm. Her childhood was idyllic and she wrote an account of it that appeared in the *Sussex County Magazine* in 1935. *A South Down Farm in the Sixties* was issued by J.M. Dent in 1938. The book provides many interesting insights into agricultural practices she also explains what home life was like on a farm in such a secluded situation. In 1872 Maude Robinson went to a private boarding school at Lewes. The school regime was Spartan but the mistresses were kindly and a good education was provided. One by one the older Robinson children moved away from Saddlescombe until, after the death of her parents, only Ernest, who ran the farm, and Maude remained. Both of them loved the downland and took an interest in its wildlife.
Paperback 210 x 148mm 82 pages 19 photos
2004 Country Books ISBN 1 898941 93 9 Price **£8.50**

THE COUNTRYMAN'S JEWEL: DAYS IN THE LIFE OF A 16th CENTURY SUSSEX SQUIRE Edited by Marcus Woodward
Facsimile of the first edition of 1934. The life of Sir Leonard Mascall of Plumpton Place. A compiler of books on country life, 'How to set stones and sow pippins' and 'The Government of Cattell'. He was farrier to the King and introduced the carp and pippin to England. The particular workes that a husbandman must be carefull to doe everie month in the yeere; the condition and state of a hus-wife; of kine & calves; the garden of pleasure or flower garden; of the honey-bee; the vertues of herbes; a discourse on Nicotian; of the manner of making stewes & pooles for fishes; the ale-house; downland sheep; oxen & horses; the barber surgeon & some gossip; sport; the farmer must have knowledge of of the things foretelling rain; knowledge of the motions of the moon.
Paperback 210 x 148mm 330 pages
2005 Country Books ISBN 1 898941 97 1 Price **£14.50**

SUSSEX FOLK AND SUSSEX WAYS by Rev John Coker Egerton
Taken from the 1923 edition with a foreword by Seila Kaye-Smith. First published 1884, the

author was rector of Burwash in the 19th century. 8 photos.

He was rector of Burwash & opens the book with this prophetic statement: 'In a few years' time the manners & customs of Sussex men, women & children will have passed away as utterly as pack-horses & stage wagons. Round frocks (smocks) will be extinct, & with them the characteristics of mind, thought, and speech which round frocks betokened. I well know the change must come, but I own that I look forward with but little satisfaction to the time when our boys & girls will all speak a uniform language prescribed by the Committee of Council on Education, & when our men & women will think only just as other people think.' He was a keen observer of the Sussex 'peasant' – "I knew she was old, Vicar, because her flannel petticoats were made of silk!" Extracts from the parish registers. Appendix: History of Burwash.

Paperback 210 x 148mm 160 pages. 8 B&W photos.

2005 Country Books ISBN 1 898941 98 X Price **£9.95**

THE STORY OF SHOREHAM by Henry Cheal

Facsimile of the first edition of 1921. The history of Shoreham from early times with references to the surrounding area, Lancing, Steyning, etc. The Saxons; the town & harbour in the Middle Ages; watermills & windmills; Old Erringham; early deeds of the Blaker, Monk & Bridger families; De Braose & De Mowbray families; fairs & markets; inns; bungalow town; suspension brudge; ancient religious houses; the ancient ferry; the Marlipins; forgotten street names; smugglers; ship building; etc. Index. Line illus by Arthur B Packham. Folding illus map.

Paperback 200 x 138mm 286 pages

2005 Country Books ISBN 1 898941 96 3 Price **£14.50**

THE SUSSEX RECIPE BOOK Edited by Dick Richardson

Recipes from a medieval manuscript from Arundel Castle, Susannah Stacey of East Chiltington and other 19th century sources. Engravings.

Paperback 210 x 148mm 120 pages

2005 Country Books ISBN 1 898941 99 8 Price **£9.95**

THE STORY OF HENFIELD by Rev Henry de Candole

A facsimile of this classic first published in 1947. The beginnings of Henfield; Saxon and Norman times; the manor of Stretham; communications – river, road and rail; the church and village in the middle ages; the Bysshopp family; Elizabeth I to the civil war; Henfield Place and the Holneys; old Henfield papers; the church in the 18th and 19th centuries; village life, trade and industries; houses, inns and schools; references, index. 9 photographs

Paperback 220 x 136mm 207 pages

2005 Ashridge Press ISBN 1 901214 48 6 Price **£14.50**

NOOKS AND CORNERS OF OLD SUSSEX by Rev P de Putron

A facsimile of this scarce book published in 1875 of choice examples of Sussex archaeology. Over 300 early-mid 19th century engravings. Churches 'restored' by the Victorians; the Star Inn at Alfriston before the timber frame was exposed; the shrine of St Lawrence at Ottenham Abbey, Henfield; old manor houses, etc. An invaluable source for those researching local or family history. The engravings lend themselves to colouring and framing.

Large paperback 295 x 205mm 160 pages

2005 Ashridge Press ISBN 1 901214 49 4 Price **£18.50**